W9-BAP-615

The Lost Cellos of Lev Aronson

Lev Aronson's Pencil Drawing of
Gregor Piatigorsky and Pablo Casals

Atlas & Co.
New York

The Lost Cellos of Lev Aronson

Frances Brent

Photograph of Lev Aronson meeting Piatigorsky used by permission
of the Queens Borough Public Library, Long Island Division, *New
York Herald-Tribune* Photo Morgue.

Excerpts from "Oral Memoirs of Daniel Arie Sternberg" printed by
permission of Baylor University, The Texas Collection, Waco, Texas.

Atlas & Co. *Publishers*
15 West 26th Street, 2nd floor
New York, NY 10010
www.atlasandco.com

Distributed to the trade by W. W. Norton & Company

Printed in the United States

Atlas & Company books may be purchased for
educational, business, or sales promotional use.
For information, please write to info@atlasandco.com.

Library of Congress Cataloging-in-Publication Data
is available upon request.

ISBN: 978-1-934633-11-3

13   12   11   10   09   1   2   3   4   5   6

This book is dedicated to the memory of Lev Aronson's first students, who died at the time of the Riga ghetto.

Where did Rothschild get that good fiddle?
Did he buy it or steal it or get it out of a pawnshop?
—Anton Chekhov

Ars longa, vita brevis.

Contents

Preface

In Chicago in the 1960s, I took lessons from a pianist who was from Prague and Vienna. She had come to the United States with her husband and their son, but her parents and sisters died in one of the death camps in Poland. In her studio there was a pair of crackled, giant, Austrian-built grand pianos which had belonged in her family's apartment when she was a child. When I played them, I heard a woolen quality; the lower registers were grainy and the higher tones almost pure percussion. The foreign sound was a reminder of the transfer of people and objects in Europe, west and east, during the Second World War. In my childhood these instruments embodied my understanding of the Holocaust: a voice and a wooden box was a metaphor for what had been saved and what was lost.

Many years later I heard the story of a string instrument, a cello that had been wrapped in oilcloth, buried in Poland during the Nazi occupation, and uncovered by a Jewish musician; I was fascinated by the outlines of his story. The musician's name was Lev Aronson. He had been a student of Gregor Piatigorsky in Berlin in the late 1920s and early 1930s. After the war he came to

America and joined the Dallas Symphony, where he was principal cellist for nearly twenty years. He must have been a remarkable teacher. His students included Lynn Harrell and Ralph Kirshbaum, as well as principals for the Chicago Symphony, the Dallas Symphony, and the Dallas Opera. In an interview, Ralph Kirshbaum described his signature voice: "He enunciated with the bow in such a way as to speak with a sound that had great character, which is something that comes from within, not from a special technique." In 1990 the Janzer Foundation honored him with the *Chevalier du violoncello*, which was received posthumously by his widow.

Although in his youth he had traveled through the music world of Europe with great expectations, for most of his life he struggled against obscurity: "My fate is probably to be known more than to be famous." Because he experienced the cultural collapse in Europe so tragically himself, he felt an intense need to continue the tradition and to pass it on. The story of the instruments that slipped through his hands provides the framework for this book, offering a way of thinking about what perished and what was saved and, of course, taking another look at the relationship of Jews to European culture. By all accounts, he was passionate about the voice of the cello, teaching his students how to listen for sound and to produce it. Even with inexpensive instruments, he insisted on respectful care. In the last years of his life, he played a cello made by Francesco Goffriller in 1725. It had a dark, profound sound, projecting out before falling down. In that way, one of his students told me, the instrument was very much like he was. "You couldn't win an argument with Lev," he said.

I've been told that in his house Lev always left one latch of his cello case undone. Asked why, he replied, "That's how it can breathe."

Chapter 1

Lost Cellos

1988

DALLAS

I feel so empty and alone—

In my dreams I have a happy life. I always hear music.

I had so much fun with the Hoax Trio as Heifetz called it. Rubinstein laughed about it and Piaty was there. The tempi were excellent—just right! It made so much sense—even with the wrong notes each added. Haydn would have liked it—in a sense it was like the Surprise Symphony—Trio #1, the Mozart Symphony conducted by Rudolph, like a fast Brahms with the Chopin coda—I had so much fun. Dreams are better than being awake—

I even conducted and liked it. It's something!

—Lev Aronson, draft of journal entry

1986

DALLAS

> *My name is Lev Aronson. . . . Born in München-*
> *Gladbach of Jewish parents in 1912. I began my*
> *musical and cello education at the age of six . . .*

The correspondence, dated 1986, is Lev's second letter
to the Federal Republic of Germany. The first, written in
1953, hadn't been answered. In 1986, he was seventy-
four years old, and he may have known as much about
playing the cello as anyone alive. He had been living in
Dallas for thirty-eight years, first in a boarding house,
then in a run-down and poorly heated bungalow near
Love Field, later in a house on Pinocchio Drive. He could
regale audiences with "fantastic stories of his colorful
past," but the telling was disjointed, contradictory, and
sometimes lacking in painful details. His English was so
garbled, even his students had trouble interpreting his
instructions: "Compact bow!" or "The train has already
left the station!" Among colleagues he was known for
his acerbic tongue: "Show me where in the score it says
'Batter the cello!'" He drove a black Cadillac sedan, was
crazy about Westerns, cooked borscht, beef Stroganoff,
and piroshki, and had a taste for vodka and beautiful
women. In his billfold he carried a *Reichsmark* ration
coupon, the ticket stub from the SS *Marine Marlin*,
and an autographed dollar. He had a companionable
parrot who spoke Russian. He kept eleven pocket-sized
leather notebooks with conversion tables, year planners,
the names of students, a few distant cousins, fellow

émigrés, and musicians ranging from Victor Babin, Raya Garbousova, Robert Hofmekler, Herman Godes, and Marc Lavry to Antal Dorati, William Pleeth, Leonard Rose, Slava Rostropovich, Isaac Stern, and Janos Starker. He preserved in an envelope the cigar that Arthur Rubinstein had given him in Switzerland. He owned a grainy, low-quality copy of *The Shop on Main Street* recorded from his television set. Forty-five years had passed since the German occupation of Riga, but the memories were with him.

In composing the letter, it must have been difficult for Lev to arrange his thoughts; his feelings were mixed together, and anything he could say would seem incomplete. At first he listed names of the dead: his parents, Pessa and Zorach Aronson; his sister Gerda; an aunt and an uncle; "as well as innumerable other relatives and their friends. . . . How I still miss my family after all these years. . . . " Twenty-five members of his father's family perished during the war.

Then he turned to the loss of livelihood, the end of his career as a soloist: "I am not sure which was more detrimental to my hands, what fatally damaged them more, the hard physical slave labor or the enforced isolation away from cello practicing. . . . " Although Lev continued to develop as an artist and musician after the war, and one might argue that his experiences in Riga and in the camps made his music deeper, he was haunted by the idea that his technical fluency had been damaged and the time for making a career had passed.

The loss of things, the most mundane of all losses, symbols of the life that once surrounded him, came last.

Lev catalogued the confiscated contents of his apartment: art and crystal, a Bechstein concert grand piano, and "my, today, priceless musical instrument collection: two cellos—a Nicholas Amati and a fine Mathias Neuner, a German maker; and two invaluable and wonderful bows—a Tourte and a Lamy, considered today to be treasures. . . . I remember how all my possessions, as well as those of my parents and relatives, were confiscated and stolen. . . . My musical instruments, my art work, my furnishings, all my papers, bills of sale and records, recordings and music . . ."

In closing he explained how he had waited between the two letters "more than forty years. . . . I felt that it was too soon after the war to burden Germany with the cost of reparations, I felt that Germany had to regain her feet economically to assist the anti-Fascist element of your society that was now reconstructing this economy, that did play a part in the defeat. . . . I felt any reparations would be insufficient anyway at that time; and I also, quite frankly, felt very proud—as though I could [not] put a compensatory price on the lives of my family. . . . It was too close to the horror. . . ." But in this document, "in the interest of fairness, ethics, justice, and international law," he calculated the value of the confiscated items, stipulating, "there is no way to value the loss of my family. . . . "

In parentheses he added, "I am convinced that somewhere in Germany or Austria someone is playing that priceless Amati cello and Tourte bow. . . ."

7 JULY 1941
RIGA

With difficulty Lev Aronson carried his cellos, bows, and cases up the stairs of the main post office. In a notebook, many years later, he wrote: "the typical wide stairs of old Russian government buildings, cold cement and steep steps, hard to handle with two cellos and emotional pain. . . . " Two Latvian auxiliary police—volunteers dressed in civilian clothes and newly issued brassards—escorted him from behind. Lev shifted his weight up the stairwell. A group of Jewish musicians, jackets over their shoulders in the heat, was already leaving. No one spoke, "but a whole world was expressed in their glances."

Since Melngalvju nams, the House of Blackheads, was destroyed in German bombing and fires on the evening of June 29, the predominantly non-Jewish radio orchestra had lost its largest instruments and most of its music library. The post office had become its headquarters. Other Jewish musicians with valuable instruments had been summoned to the radio station. Lists of their names had been obtained from Latvian collaborators. Everyone milled around in a daze in the large postal room. Cases were opened; bows and instruments were lifted off velvet and satin linings. Outside, there was a great deal of commotion: Hundreds of people were in the streets. German cars made their way through the roads while vigilantes crowded the neighborhoods, leading small processions of startled Jews. Inside it was quiet enough to hear the ping of vibrating strings.

Someone hastily pushed Lev forward with his aluminum and leather cases, and the principal cellist of the radio orchestra, a man he knew well, approached. Lev was nearly six feet tall. He was accustomed to thinking of himself as "a man of the world," but he was disoriented in the unusual setting. The man who was facing him, a well-known musician and a colleague, was not a common criminal like the thugs in the streets. He nodded awkwardly in greeting before Lev reluctantly unlatched and opened the lids of the cases.

When Lev released the instruments from their ties, it was the last time he touched the beautiful spiral, the seahorse tail of the Amati scroll. The cellist, his old colleague, smiled, shifting his gaze to the window. Then, turning his back, "his meaning was clear."

Something lunatic caused Lev to ask a question. He chose his words in German, the current language of the street, rather than Russian, which would have been used ten days earlier: "Can I have a receipt?" The room filled with laughter. Lev felt a hand clutch the collar of his coat, shoving him backward, down the stairs.

Chapter 2

From Jewish Life

A LOST WORLD

I'm listening to a recording Lev Aronson made with the organist Joyce Jones in 1971, Bloch's *Prayer*. There's nothing hectic in the interpretation, just a remnant sweetness followed by profound sadness. The phrasing is meditative, one feels the pulse; the upper ranges are fluid and full-bodied. The snake charmer passages are played with a restrained spirituality even when the score plumbs to the bottom C. In certain registers the sound Lev produces matches the organ's tone, but his shifts are vocal, informed by the memory of Jewish liturgical music from his childhood in Voronezh and Riga and, later, his friendship with the cantorially trained lyric tenor Joseph Schmidt.

Bloch's composition *From Jewish Life* was intended to evoke the beautiful lost world of Jewry. Written before the war, it's an idealized vision commemorating the passing of a culture and its long-suffering people. There would be few people with better credentials than Lev Aronson to act as intermediary between that vanished world with all its defects and ours. Lev was born in 1912. His family came from the duchy of Kurland, the brim of land bordering Lithuania to the south, the Baltic Sea to the west, and the Gulf of Riga to the North. Their city had four names: Mitava (Russian), Mitau (German), Jelgava (Latvian), Mitoi (Yiddish). It was a river city with narrow sidewalks, somber shops, and cobblestone streets, dusty in the summer, misty and flooded with rain and snow in the winter. Like in other provincial cities, children played games on the roads where vendors carted bushels of oats and carried milk jars on their backs. In the muddy market square there were cattle and carts, horses wearing feed sacks, ragged boot-makers, fishmongers, rabbit farmers, tanners, open stalls for dry goods and woven rugs, booths where chickens were hung by the neck.

As in much of the Baltic area, the town had been conquered and settled by Germans in the thirteenth century, and German culture and language remained the predominant influence even after it became a Polish duchy in the sixteenth century and was annexed to Russia at the end of the eighteenth century. The city was known for its marvelous Rastrelli Palace, the ducal residence with hundreds of jewel-like windows, balconies, French gardens, clipped green hedges, and roses. Before the railroad lines were built, Mitava was the connecting point between Vilna, Vitebsk, and Riga, but by the turn of the century it was only a link on the way to the larger port cities. In 1897 there were 6,000 Jews within the general population of 35,000, which included German Balts, Poles, Lithuanians, Russians, and the Letts. For the most part, each group kept to itself, mutually bewildered by the others. They might meet for business and sometimes in school, but there were few close social contacts. The Jews would have included German-speaking Baltic Jews who understood Yiddish but might not have spoken it at home as did Jews from White Russia and Lithuania, who had the opportunity to acquire greater wealth and deeper knowledge of Hebrew and Yiddish. By 1914 the population had grown to 45,000, and the Jewish community increased proportionately. The main synagogue, Die grosse Synagoge, was capped with an onion-shaped cupola.

From the mid-nineteenth century Jews were well established in the economy of Mitava. They worked as bankers and doctors—there was a Jewish hospital—innkeepers, merchants, and craftsmen. The record book, *Pinkas Hakehillot*, of the Jewish communities of Latvia and Estonia lists the following professions: "hatters, furriers, tailors and seamstresses, salesgirls, shoemakers, goldsmiths, tinsmiths, watchmakers, locksmiths, opticians, painters and sign painters, engravers, glaziers, carpenters, coachmen, butchers, and ritual slaughterers." Predictably, they filled the role of "middlemen" in the grain and textile businesses and horse dealers. The less well-off were "peddlers, cabmen, porters, wood choppers, and water drawers."

Daily life at the turn of the century must have been similar to the one described by Robert Herzenberg, from Libau to the west where Lev eventually was the principal cellist in the philharmonic: "In school there were fewer Letts than Jews, we were good schoolmates [*kameraden*] but there was no closer contact. . . . The special distinguishing feature [*characteristicum*] was the stability [*bestandigkeit*] of the world. Who could doubt the permanence of the Romanovs, the Hohenzollern and the Habsburger. . . . Life was beautiful [*shoen*] and one had everything. Goods were especially cheap; a full-grown goose cost one ruble. . . . We had to eat the expensive kosher beef and lamb, which cost 18–20 kopeks per pound. . . . There were smoked sprats, herring, flounder, and salmon. In winter only the latter was available, but in summer the market was flooded with the best and cheapest berries and fruit . . . and strawberries from the garden; blueberries . . . apples, pears, nuts, cherries, etc. The time for making preserves came in the fall, and for weeks there was cooking of juices, and preserves for winter, since until early summer there would be nothing fresh except potatoes and beets. . . . Clothing was expensive since there were no ready-to-wear items. The tailor measured for everything and brought the cloth and accessories . . . the shoemaker came to the house. . . . The winters were quite cold; already in the fall one would buy several cords of birch wood. . . . Only in the spring would the storm windows [*winter rahmen*] be put away again. . . . "

Lev's maternal grandfather was a klezmer—as he put it, "an unschooled country fiddler who played for weddings, Bar Mitzvahs, and funeral parties." Other members of his mother's family were also musicians. A distant cousin, Nikolai Arnoff, was a professional cellist. Lev's paternal grandfather, Wulff Aronson, like thousands of other

Jewish boys, had been taken forcibly from his home when he was twelve years old and conscripted by Russian soldiers as part of Tsar Nicholas's attempt to convert children of the Jewish poor to Russian Orthodoxy. Children like him were described by Alexander Herzen as he saw them in Vyatka: "Pale, worn out, with frightened faces, they stood in thick, clumsy soldier's overcoats, with stand-up collars, fixing helpless, pitiful eyes on the garrison soldiers who were roughly getting them into ranks. . . . " Like many of the others, Wulff Aronson spent a quarter of a century in the Russian military and never saw his parents again. When he returned home he dutifully reestablished himself in the community as a merchant and tailor.

Lev's parents, a tailor and a seamstress, were also amateur musicians. His mother "played the piano and sang Schubert lieder." His father played a violin which had been a wedding gift from his father-in-law—in Lev's words: "He gave him a violin and told him what to do with it. He was his first and only teacher." As a couple, they must have had an adventurous streak. After Wulff's death, they obtained travel documents and went with their infant son to Berlin, the heart of musical and industrial Europe. Zorach enrolled in the *Fachhoschule*—School of Fashion Design—in order to master the trade he inherited. They lived as young people always have done, in sordid outskirts of the city, absorbing what they could of the concert halls, theaters, monuments, gardens, long-faced palaces, wide brownstone houses, and lacy iron pavilions. They attended recitals by Bronislaw Huberman and Mischa Ellman. From the high decks of the concert hall they listened to Ysaÿe's poetic performances of Fauré and Saint-Saëns.

In the spring of 1911 their small son developed a fever. The distraught young couple "knocked at every door, asking for help." They were looking for a German doctor, but no one was willing to treat the child of impoverished Jewish students. By the time a doctor from the Jewish welfare organization came to their flat, "cursing all his colleagues," the baby's pneumonia had progressed, and he died. A year later, Lev was born in the border town of München-Gladbach while his mother was visiting a friend. Within a few weeks Zorach completed his coursework and the young family returned to Kurland.

With knowledge of materials, imported fabrics, and the newest sewing techniques, Zorach took charge of the family business, a tailor's shop in Mitava. As a prosperous merchant, he acted as lawyer and banker for Jewish townsmen who kept cash savings in his store. Things went well enough that he was able to return to Germany for a "cure" to relieve a childhood injury to his leg. That was where he was in the summer of 1914 when the Archduke Franz Ferdinand was assassinated. With trains suddenly converted for military use, it took weeks for him to return home, sailing from Sweden to Norway and Finland, then making his way down to Petrograd and Riga to Mitava. There must have been music making in the young household when the large family, perhaps thirty relatives, turned out to celebrate his homecoming as well as the birth of a daughter, but six months later Mitava was inundated with war refugees and wounded soldiers. On April 18, 1915, they received the Decree of Expulsion. The German army was advancing and Russia was scapegoating the Jewish population for humiliating war losses. The Jews of Kurland were allowed twenty-four hours (then as a reprieve they were given forty-eight) to prepare to leave their homes. In the following days, nearly 40,000 Jews were deported east on long lines of trains that had been sent to the provincial stations.

Families crowded onto the cattle cars—babies and teenagers, porters, doctors, imbeciles, the elderly, pregnant women, cripples. Forty people were jammed in each carriage guarded by Russian soldiers. Around them on the straw floor, their remaining possessions lay bundled in sacks made of feather beds tied with rope—clothes and bedding, chamber pots, metal teapots, toys, soothers, precious collections of ritual objects and musical instruments. There was pandemonium in the station. The cars had neither steps nor ladders. Small children and invalids were lifted up by their legs and arms. After several hours the doors closed and the train began to move toward Riga. The refugees watched a small square of sky through the iron grate covering an opening near the ceiling. Through planks of the cattle cars they saw the familiar landscape recede: low-lying green fields, pine forests and bogs, market towns that smelled of wet grass and manure. Some had purposefully left their houses open, an acknowledgment that what was left behind would surely be looted. Others had given a few possessions to Latvian neighbors or buried them in the ground.

The train made many stops—in Riga, Dvinsk, Vitebsk, Mogilev, and other cities where the local Jewish communities crowded to the stations with "sugar, cheese and herring, eggs, boiled meat" to feed the unfortunate travelers. Through the wet and misty distance, Lev listened to the chugging rhythm of the train, the occasional moaning of its horn as a bombardment of shells exploded in the distance. He was three years old and this was his first memory: "As I'm trying to remember the early days of my life, there are two things that come to mind: the sound of a moving train and the sound of artillery shells. . . . "

The Jews were dispersed south and east in the provinces of Chernigov, Poltava, and Ekaterinoslav. The Aronson family unloaded in Voronezh, about five hundred kilometers from Moscow. It was a gloomy city on the upper Don, bare and cold, with seemingly endless fields, the hunting grounds for the family of the tsar. There was already a drafty brick synagogue built in basilica form by the small community of Jewish pharmacists, lawyers, doctors, and shopkeepers who had come before them. At first the refugees were settled in an enclave of the Jewish community, in houses made of bare wood planks, heated by iron ovens lit with kerosene. Water ran off the roofs and down the walls, collecting into barrels when it rained. Somehow, in those bewildering and primitive surroundings, Zorach formed a partnership with another tailor and began the arduous process of repairing his life.

What was the musical world of these faraway provinces? In interior Russia, there had long been ensembles of horns and parlor orchestras with conglomerations of other instruments: French horn, violin, bassoon, flute, and cymbal. Smaller orchestras might include balalaikas, guitars, and drums. Theater clubs and army units had brass bands with cornets, horns, tubas, and annotated bass drums. Gypsies would come through with the instruments collected from their wanderings—sometimes leading a ragged dancing bear on hind legs, clawless, teeth filed to stubs, iron ring pierced through its nose, a tambourine held gingerly between its paws as if it were a large biscuit or porcelain plate.

Across the mosaic of Eastern European Jewish communities, there were three great traditions: cantorial music, klezmer, and Yiddish songs. With the modern age, the Jewish communities in cities like Odessa, Berdichev, and Vilna produced any number of hazzans, coloratura tenors. They not only sang in synagogues but gave concerts and made recordings. Some of the vocalists went to the conservatories and eventually—like Lev's good friend Joseph Schmidt—sang on the stage, in opera, or in movies. On the other hand, Jewish klezmer orchestras provided a link in fragilely divided Russian village society, since they performed for Jewish celebrations as well as for gentile peasants and gentry.

In 1908, the *Gezelshaft far Yiddisher Folks-Muzik* (Society for Jewish Folk Music, established in St. Petersburg but with branches in outlying cities, including Riga) began to collect and transcribe Jewish music from the Russian empire. Their findings included instrumental music such as Jewish wedding dances and celebration pieces, cantorial work, traditional holiday songs, Sabbath songs, wordless Hasidic tunes, and nursery folk songs first sung in the shtetls. There was also more modern choral music arranged for the choral synagogues, where men and boys in the balconies would sing antiphonally to the cantor, and there were new compositions for orchestra and chamber players based on traditional Jewish melodies and tropes. The Society sponsored lectures and concerts, and their publication of sheet music was received with enthusiasm. At the start of the First World War, Mitava was one of several regional centers for the Society. The refugees from Kurland would have brought with them songs and choral music inspired by the Jewish renaissance. The Jewish community in Voronezh hosted concerts for the Society.

Many Jewish musicians established themselves in the broader culture of European music. In Russia, almost half of the students in the St. Petersburg Conservatory were Jewish, and Jews comprised nearly eighty percent of the enrollment in the Odessa Conservatory. Professionally trained, virtuosic Jewish string players, pianists, composers, and conductors were esteemed throughout the Russian empire, and Jewish wind players distinguished themselves in the military bands and orchestras (and later in jazz ensembles). Some of these musicians were children of klezmer musicians or had been apprenticed to cantors. Others came from the growing secularized Jewish middle class. In the small cities, Jewish and gentile musicians might play together in local concert groups formed of bakers, tanners, watchmakers, as well as members of the firemen's brigade or the doctors' orchestras; and it was common to have chamber performances in homes and apartments.

How were instruments obtained? At first string instruments had been made locally and passed through families (the Yiddish riddle goes: "Do you want to know how many men there are in a house? Look on the walls! As many fiddles as hang there—that's how many men!"), shared with friends, used as barter, or pawned for debt. As a boy, Piatigorsky claimed to have found a cello in a vegetable market: "it was coal black, and it had wormholes and many cracks that were cemented or roughly repaired with carpenter's glue. The varnish had a smell of tar. . . . " But in modern times things were different. Stores stocked string instruments and pianos constructed in the factories of St. Petersburg as well as the workshops in Saxony, Bohemia, and Moravia. Brass horns, trumpets, cornets, flutes, serpentine tubas, or euphoniums might have been acquired by the conscripted youth assigned to military bands and carried wearily home, tied at the waist or on a cord around the neck. They were also imported from Julius Heinrich Zimmermann's brass and woodwind shops.

1917
VORONEZH

In Voronezh there was a very rich family near the place where we lived. They had three children. Borya, Gitscha, and Anya were the names of the children.

They all played ... violin, cello, and piano. And I was sitting there sometimes under the window listening to it, trying to grasp. The boy that played cello came to me and showed me the bow. I had a funny feeling when I took the bow.... "What's that big instrument? What do you call it?" I had a funny feeling that I would like to have an instrument like that. "This isn't for poor people, immigrants, like you. It's for rich, good Christians," he said.

Lev Aronson described his introduction to the cello with a story that contained two parts, a troubled dream and a resolution: Not long after the encounter with Borya, the cellist Nikolai Arnoff arrived in Voronezh. He came to give a concert and stayed with the Aronson family as a guest. When Arnoff heard the story about the Russian boy, he handed Lev his cello and said, "Play it." He made room for the boy to sit beside him and showed him how to position the big instrument between his legs and how to "draw" the bow. Arnoff may have played some of the show pieces—Popper's *Tarantelle* or *Hungarian Rhapsodie*—as well as the new compositions like Leo Zeitlin's *Eli Zion*, the Hebraic-sounding voice dipping below baritone and then rising in longing like a lullaby. The music made a deep impression. After Arnoff left, Zorach took his son to an instrument shop and purchased a small-sized cello.

1918

VORONEZH

Aron Rafaelovitsch Rubinstein, a fellow emigrant from Kurland, was Lev's first cello teacher. He was also the teacher of Nikolai Graudan, future principal cellist for the Berlin Philharmonic. But music lessons didn't last long. In the spring of 1918 the Whites entered Voronezh Province, and Lev saw three Russian generals with his own eyes: Anton Ivanovich Denikin, Roman Fyodorovich Ungern von Sternberg, and Andrei Grigoriyevich Shkuro, head of the anti-Bolshevik Cossacks and then the cavalry under Denikin. Shkuro traveled in a car that was painted with the picture of a wolf on the door. The wolf's mouth was open wide, exposing huge and grotesque teeth. Underneath were the words: BAI JIDI SPASAI RUSSIA, "Kill the Jews and Save Russia." Cossack cavalrymen descended on the city and the Aronson children ran from the cellar to a yard where they were "buried up to their stomachs in manure." From that vantage point they saw their father struck across the face with a whip and an elderly, observant Jew strapped on the back of a horse. Barbed wire was wound around the old man's neck. When its hindquarters were slapped with a stick, the horse lunged forward and the bearded old man was decapitated.

Lev remembered with irony his initial enthusiasm for the Revolution and its sweeping education reforms, the simplification of Russian spelling and removal of obsolete letters, which was a relief for school children. But when the Bolsheviks arrived, they routed the city again. This time Jews were rounded up as counter-revolutionaries and Lev's father was taken to prison, where he remained until an epidemic of typhus fever swept through and he was released to come staggering home with the disease. While the family tended to him, Lev's mother and aunt developed the mulberry rash and fever. The baby Gerda was sent to another Jewish family, but Lev remained to take care of the sick. In the bitter cold, he stole logs to make a fire in the iron stove and dug potatoes and turnips from the fields. When the others recovered, he also came down with the fever.

The following year the family was given permission to return to Latvia. Most of the Jewish property in Mitava had been looted or destroyed by fighting, first between Russians and Germans and then between Bolsheviks and Latvians. The Aronsons chose to go to Riga, where Zorach's sister was already settled. At the border, soldiers robbed them of all their belongings. The small-sized cello might have been left in Voronezh with beds and cradle or snatched by border guards with household goods, jewelry, and rubles.

Chapter 3

The Student

9 FEBRUARY 1960
BOSTON

> *My Dear Levushka,*
> *With some delay but great gladness I congratulate*
> *you on your birthday. From my whole heart and soul*
> *I wish you happiness—joy—and many years of healthy*
> *life. I got two of your letters and, as usual, I was deeply*
> *touched by your friendship and warmth.*
>
> *Thanks, my dear, I thank you both for the hospitality*
> *and also give my greetings to all your friends. . . .*
>
> *I embrace you always,*
> *Grisha*
>
> *P.S. I am not angry with ———. He did not want*
> *to do me harm. And, just to think how many people*
> *were in our lives who purposefully and maliciously*
> *abused us. But where are they? I cannot help but thank*
> *God that so little malice remains in me against them.*

Even when Lev was in his seventies, he thought of himself
as a student of Piatigorsky. The two musicians, born nine
years apart and deeply bonded in friendship, had a lot

in common. Both were immersed in the flowering of Russian-Yiddish culture which had begun at the fin de siècle. Both had witnessed pogroms in their childhoods. At different times, they had studied with the same revered teachers from the German and Russian cello schools: Julius Klengel in Leipzig and Alfred von Glehn from Moscow (though Lev worked with von Glehn in Berlin). But their temperaments, gifts, and fates were vastly different. From the very beginning, Piatigorsky demonstrated prodigious talent, strength, and vitality. He performed as an itinerant musician to support his family when he was just a child, receiving a scholarship to the Moscow Conservatory when he was only nine years old. By the time he was fifteen, he was already principal cellist of the Bolshoi Opera Orchestra and a member of what would soon be called the Lenin Quartet. With his artistic ease and profound sound, so full of life—as Lev put it, "musical . . . beautiful . . . and full of messages"—it didn't take long for him to establish a solo career. Late in life Piatigorsky was almost baffled with the blessings that fell at his feet: "It's strange; the less I feel I deserve some reward, the more I collect various medals, diplomas, citations, etc."

Lev, the son of a persevering businessman, came to music more slowly, with self-consciousness, with his intellect, and with his heart. Perhaps to make up for lost time, he chose to stay in Europe after many musicians had emigrated. During the war years, the memory of his time as a student of the famous cellist helped him withstand the humiliations of the camps. After the war, in America, Lev depended upon his teacher for entry into the sometimes harsh professional world of music. When his personal affairs didn't go well, his relationship to Piatigorsky continued to provide stability. The teacher wrote his student in 1961: "I am very worried about your tour: promise and swear to me that you will truly look after yourself. Don't force yourself, and keep the brakes on your temperamental emotions." Two years before he died, Lev told a Dallas journalist: "My teenage idol was? My teacher, Gregor Piatigorsky. The person who had the most impact on my life was? Gregor Piatigorsky."

1920

RIGA

Using political connections from his years in Mitava, Zorach Aronson established his business for a third time. As a tailor and furrier, he specialized in making women's coats, jackets, and stoles. He employed clerks to work in the shop, which catered to a rich clientele. Riga was an elegant city with steeples and spires, pillbox art nouveau buildings, and tile roofs reflected over water. The boulevards facing the parks were wide enough to accommodate carts, carriages with horses, bicycles, and automobiles. Rowboats were moored in the canal flowing through the center of the city. Shops with broad windows and painted wooden shutters were stocked with modern manufactured goods: gramophones, sewing machines, and bicycles. On the side streets inexpensive dry goods were hung in open stalls. Riga was relatively hospitable to the Jews, whose population increased from 25,000 in 1920 to 44,000 in 1935, about eleven percent of the city. As in Mitava, there was a mixture of cultures—Russian, Polish, German, Jewish, Latvian, Lithuanian, Estonian—and a certain amount of tolerance. Everyone in the community was identified according to ethnic origins, and children were given the opportunity to attend schools of their nationalities, though not forced to do so. Lev continued his education in Russian and under a quota system qualified for admission to a preeminent school, Lomonosov's Gymnasium.

With a sense of well-being, Zorach organized a society of tailors and a vocational school that taught less-advantaged young people how to cut patterns. Remembering his struggles in Berlin and Voronezh, he helped establish insurance, financial support, and welfare for Jewish immigrants. The Aronson family remained orthodox, keeping the dietary laws and attending synagogue. In the spring they continued the custom of Passover housecleaning. In the synagogue Zorach sang the Jewish chorals, traditional songs and new compositions, some written by Solomon Rosowsky, who had established Riga's Jewish Conservatory after the war. Like others from the modern generation, the family was acculturated; they identified with their religion and "took anti-Semitism for granted" but were determined not to be isolated or held back by it. They took the children to *The Barber of Seville,* the Salamonskis Circus, and the Yiddish Theater with its Jewish orchestra. Zorach "could quote Shakespeare, Tolstoy, Dostoevsky, Twain, Hugo,

Maupassant, Moliere, Cicero, Sholem Aleichem." The family spoke German, Yiddish, and Russian at home. Lev learned Hebrew in religious school and Romance languages and even some English at the gymnasium. When they lived in Mitava, the only use for Lettish would have been in the marketplace or in conversation with unskilled workers, servants, and drivers. This was different in Riga, where Lettish was one of the three languages used in parliament (German and Russian were the other two). They spent their summers at a modest dacha in Jurmala on the Baltic shore with its famous beaches, Victorian hotels, nightclubs, and band shells.

When he returned to music, Lev played the familiar minuets and bagpipe tunes on a student instrument. Throughout Europe there were hundreds of thousands of similar instruments imported from Mittenwald or Markneukirchen, modeled on the paradigms established by Stradivari, Guarneri, and Jacob Stainer, some dating back to the seventeenth century, when Matthias Klotz established his workshop. Over the years and with use, such instruments grew more resonant, adjusting to the idiosyncrasies of their owners, the world around them, and changes of seasons. Like other teenagers with musical backgrounds, Lev's first public performance was at the movies, playing for tips and the opportunity to see silent films. In a six-man orchestra led by the violinist Gregory Fomin, he played at the Splendid Palace, a neo-Baroque movie palace—the exterior decorated with angels blowing horns.

RIGA
1926

Paul Berkowitsch, perhaps the most prominent cellist in Riga, was a physician who received his medical education at Tartu University but studied music at the conservatory in St. Petersburg and in Leipzig with Julius Klengel. From 1926 through 1929 he was the principal cellist in the Latvian National Opera Orchestra and also played in chamber groups. When Lev asked Berkowitsch to give him lessons, he became the physician's only cello student. Berkowitsch and his wife, who played the harp, were childless, and lessons were conducted at four o'clock in the afternoon in their parlor. Berkowitz was a man of discipline and punctuality: "Without discipline we cannot have music. Music is not chaos." When he walked into the room, taking off his white coat, replacing it with a suit jacket, Berkowitsch efficiently shifted from doctor to musician.

Lev was with Berkowitsch when he first heard Gregor Piatigorsky perform. The recital was at the Stadttheater, the Riga Opera House, and Piatigorsky, already the principal cellist of the Berlin Philharmonic under Furtwängler, had begun to establish a reputation for his charismatic performances. From the balcony, Lev saw "a tall, slender, very handsome young man come on stage and elegantly acknowledge the applause." What he heard—the Locatelli Sonata, the Dvorak Concerto accompanied by Ivan Suchov, and clapping so loud "it seemed as though the roof of the Opera House would come off"—changed his life.

STUDY OF LAW

Lev was admitted to the University of Berlin to study law when he was only sixteen years old. Berkowitsch, who was fond of quoting Schopenhauer—"Music is the melody whose text is the world"—approved.

Lev had been influenced by two famous court cases. In 1911, Mendel Beilis, superintendent of a brick factory in Kiev, the Jewish father of five children, was accused falsely of murdering a thirteen-year-old Christian boy as blood libel with the aid of "undiscovered persons." The Beilis trial in 1913 attracted world attention because it presented the opportunity for Russian intelligentsia, including Gorky and Blok, to protest Russian anti-Semitism. The most prominent lawyers in Russia argued both sides of the case and, in the end, Beilis was acquitted. The second case involved Shalom Schwarzbard, a Jewish anarchist who made his living repairing watches and clocks. Fifteen members of his family had been killed in the pogroms in the Ukraine from 1905 to 1907. In Paris in 1926 Schwarzbard assassinated Symon Petlura, head of the exiled government of the Ukrainian People's Republic, holding him responsible for the pogroms. Miraculously, a French court took Schwarzbard's side and acquitted him after he had served in La Santé Prison for almost a year and a half.

Just as the conservatory system had once presented an opportunity for integration into the framework of Russian society, many Jews in the new generation saw the European legal system as an avenue for assimilation and justice. The judgment in both cases gave them some hope for a better future. Lev, who had lived through the expulsion from Mitava and the atrocities in Voronezh, thought he'd like to contribute to the development of new liberties.

AUTUMN 1928
BERLIN

Lev must have appeared an easy target at the Friedrich-strasse Station, "full of anticipation for what the future had in store." He wore a new suit and a long green coat. He carried the cello under his arm, a suitcase in one hand and, in the other, a basket with cigarettes and delicacies packed by his mother. Like other young men from the provinces, he was overwhelmed by the "ocean" of electric bulbs, the fountains of light, the commotion of Berlin's crowds: jugglers, acrobats, wounded war veterans, Jewish musicians, White Russian refugees, gypsy musicians, streetwalkers with teasers, transvestites, lesbians dressed in trousers—smoking—holding their girls "tight under the arms while walking in manly steps."

When evening approached and he hadn't found a hotel room, Lev made the cardinal mistake of accepting help from a stranger. An over-friendly young man offered to bring him to an inexpensive room in the outskirts of the city. They walked first under the pale yellow illumination of streetlamps and then through arched entrances and the dark maze of alleys to tenement courtyards and, finally, a hotel where the concierge led him to a bed and he quickly fell asleep. The next morning, the same boy came to his room and, as Lev put it, "began making advances while I was still in bed." Somehow Lev fended him off—"I used all my intelligence to get out of there and onto the street," winding his way back with his suitcase, basket, and cello.

WINTER 1928
BERLIN

At the university, Lev attended lectures on law and studied Latin. He took forensic anatomy, paying visits to the morgue, where gruesome, half-draped and naked cadavers were arranged on stretchers. It was a terrible sight for a sixteen-year-old boy and provided tragic foreshadowing of things to come. Lev had second thoughts about studying law but didn't want to cause concern for his parents, who had sacrificed so much on their children's behalf. Before coming to Berlin, he had envisioned "standing in front of the court and making fiery speeches, defending a victim," but this was entirely different.

One evening as he was passing through a university building, he heard music coming from one of the halls. Lev paused, pushed open the door, and saw an orchestra rehearsing inside. He entered the large lecture room, continuing to listen. With music all around, he was flooded with thoughts of home. When the orchestra stopped for a break, Lev approached one of the cellists, asking, "What kind of orchestra is this?"

The man who was facing him, Dr. Ferdinand Levi, was

the principal cellist of the Doctors Orchestra of Berlin. Lev was startled at the coincidence, finding another cellist-physician. Dr. Levi was curious about the boy's background in Riga and his musical education. Handing over his instrument, he asked Lev to play. Lev sat down, adjusted the endpin, and began a passage from the Third Goltermann Concerto, working his fingers through the runs. Levi was attentive. "Young man," he said, "continue your musical studies. Don't assume the cello will interfere with law. I'm a doctor, and the cello fits well with life in medicine. You must meet my friend Julius Klengel in Leipzig." When Lev hesitated, his new friend added an enticement that couldn't be turned down: "I'll take you in my Mercedes."

1929

LEIPZIG

By the time Lev went to him, Klengel was nearly seventy years old. He had instructed students from around the world, many extraordinary musicians: Guilhermina Suggia, Emanuel Feuermann, Mischa Schneider, Gregor Piatigorsky, and, later, William Pleeth. Professorial but kindly, Klengel wore an old-fashioned, formal suit with a high-collared shirt, and his beard was trimmed like Garibaldi's. He told Lev about his own father, who had been a lawyer and amateur musician. He listened carefully when the boy played, explaining the repertoire that would help him open up his sound. Lev liked him immediately and decided he would try some lessons. For the first few weeks Dr. Levi brought him in the Mercedes, but soon Lev went by train on his own, and ultimately he became so involved with music that he decided to leave the university and the law.

After a year, Klengel was no longer able to maintain his teaching schedule, so Lev went to the Klindworth-Scharwenka Conservatory in Berlin, taking lessons with Alfred von Glehn, who had come from the Moscow Conservatory. Von Glehn had once been a student of Davidov, the man Tchaikovsky had called "the czar of cellists." He and his wife took Lev under their wing, taking him to cafés with their daughter or inviting him to their apartment for meals. But, within the year, von Glehn died. At his funeral, students played Klengel's *Hymnus*, the solemn dissolving chords written for cello choir. The piece was an homage to their teacher and the expressive depth of the cello's sound. At the graveside Lev noticed a large, ribboned wreath with the inscription: "To my beloved teacher from his humble student, Gregor Piatigorsky."

1930

BERLIN

Piatigorsky was selected to take over von Glehn's class, and Lev was overjoyed at the thought of studying with the magnificent young cellist.

On the day of the first class, the room filled with more than a dozen young men and a young woman, several from Klengel's studio in Leipzig. The custodian of the conservatory entered the classroom, "dressed in a black coat with a lyre on each lapel to denote his authority." He called, "Silence, Mr. Gregor Piatigorsky is here!" and Piatigorsky entered, tall and handsome, "in gray striped pants and an ascot." He didn't carry a cello but walked with authority to the piano.

Many of the students, including Robert Hofmekler from Vilna and Jasha Bernstein, were older than Lev, closer to Piatigorsky in age. They had all been friends in Leipzig, and some already had begun to establish their careers as musicians. In a mixture of German, Russian, and Yiddish, the class greeted Piatigorsky with too much familiarity.

After a pause, Piatigorsky said: "This is a conservatory, and I'm the professor of cello. Whoever doesn't want to study is free to leave immediately, faster the better. Our old relationship has no bearing on this one. We can be colleagues and friends after class, but here I'm the professor and you're the students. If you don't want to study, you can go. I'll leave the classroom so you can make a decision. I'll be back in ten minutes. I expect a different atmosphere in this class."

Lev was astonished by Piatigorsky's confidence and authority. Some of the students left but a core remained, and when Piatigorsky returned, the class began. Piatigorsky started the class by listening to Robert Hofmekler perform. Then he played on Hofmekler's cello, releasing the bright and colorful sound he was listening for. Hofmekler was the son of a well-known cellist, and he was prepared to learn from the demonstration. The second student was Luisa Mueller, and though she was a gifted musician she didn't play to her ability. This gave Piatigorsky the opportunity to talk about some of the fundamentals. Lev was the third student. He chose the Second Romberg Concerto. He had been working on it with von Glehn, but suddenly it seemed impossible— "Playing for these giants was like playing for the entire world." His performance was mediocre. He struggled to keep the notes in tune, maintaining his sound, but couldn't make the instrument talk. Piatigorsky asked to see Lev's cello. He picked it up and began playing with a mixture of decisiveness and insight Lev hadn't come close to achieving.

After class, while Lev was packing up, Piatigorsky drew him aside: "You've got a decent instrument. What do you think about the piece?"

"I understand it but I can't do it myself. I try to play with imagination . . . "

"What do you want to do?" Piatigorsky asked.

Suddenly all Lev could think about was the disastrous decision to leave law school: "I want to commit suicide!"

Piatigorsky replied, "Do you? Oh, that's good. How will you do it? I've got so many ideas. Do you have a pharmacist? You'll take poison? But that's so unpleasant. You want to shoot yourself? But there's blood all over the place. Do you have a cord? Hang yourself! Or, wait, can you swim? No? That's very good. I'll take you to a bridge. You'll drown very quickly!"

They walked until they reached the river and crossed onto a bridge. Lev looked down into the water and

Piatigorsky said, "Maybe it's not a good day for drowning." He paused, "Now tell me something about yourself." When he heard Lev was from Riga, he launched into one of his improbable stories: He had been swindled, he said, when he played at the Riga Opera House. He had arrived in the city without money, only enough to buy a packet of the local delicacy, "*Rakovije Sheiky*, lobster necks, marvelous candies with chocolate inside." The next morning, anticipating payment, he began eating the candies, unwrapping them one by one from their beautiful colored papers. When the candies were gone, he looked for the booking agent, Mr. Serechevsky. He inquired in the hotel lobby. "Mr. Serechevsky? He's been here and gone. He's left this envelope for you, a third-class train ticket from Riga to Berlin." And Piatigorsky remembered that just as he got on the train and it started to move, there was the little man, Mr. Serechevsky, waving from behind a column.

1931

BERLIN

After the war, Lev looked back on the Berlin years in disbelief. Concert posters were stapled to the kiosks on street corners with the names of Emil Sauer, Artur Schnabel, Nathan Milstein, Claudio Arrau, Moritz Rosenthal, and the child prodigy Yehudi Menuhin. There was a piano virtuoso, Vladimir de Pachmann, who would engage in dialogue with himself while he performed. Everyone crowded to his concerts to hear the eccentric way he groaned and scolded on stage: "Oh Pachmann, you played that very badly. Let's try it one more time!" Furtwangler conducted the Philharmonic. Leo Blech, Erich Kleiber, Otto Klemperer, and Richard Strauss conducted at the opera houses. Movie palaces, theaters, the Yiddish theater, political cabarets, variety revues, bars, and hotels were filled with music. On the sidewalks there were military bands and organ grinders with monkeys. In the clubs there was American-style jazz with piano, trumpets, horns, trombones, and the "Jewish" instrument, the saxophone. Flamboyantly dressed gypsies played in the cafés, and students of classical music watched and learned from their freedom of movement and expressiveness. The city was awash in instruments—organs, harps, accordions, banjos, snare drums, vibraphones. In the Tiergarten, Russian immigrants stowed their instruments beneath benches where they slept. In the tenement courtyards, Hasidic refugees played accordions for a few pfennig.

Lev became devoted to Piatigorsky, with his unconventional teaching style, "not so much . . . solving immediate problems but . . . looking ahead . . . caring for the whole person and not merely the cellist," and it became a model he would strive for in later years. Piatigorsky took Lev to bookstalls, suggesting authors— Schiller, Goethe, Heine, Hegel, Schopenhauer, Kant. He bought books for the boy and sometimes meals. Piatigorsky had lived during the hunger and rationing in Moscow and was concerned that his student was thin. He insisted they go together to the restaurant where Lev took his meals, "about twenty-five cents for a dinner and the soup was like water." While they ate together, he wanted to know if Lev went to museums, what painters he liked, and what he had learned in law school.

The young cellists in his class, Luisa Mueller, Max Messig, and a Lithuanian boy named Buninsky, made progress with his advice: "Do what I say. . . . If you don't do what I say, you'll never play. . . . Do what I say and play exactly, precisely. . . . Start listening to yourself. . . . Develop your inner ear. . . . Through your inner ear you'll play. One doesn't play with fingers and bow. You play with your insides, with your mind, you're transforming, involved! Now, I hear only notes. I don't want notes, I want to hear playing. . . . Sing, sing . . . make a big aria . . . sing on the instrument. Play lots of short pieces, it's very important. . . ."

While Piatigorsky was on tour, he arranged for other cellists such as Joseph Schuster and Enrico Mainardi to teach his students. When he returned, he was fascinated by the techniques his colleagues had introduced. In particular, Mainardi had shown the class a different way of using their fingers on the frog of the bow. By keeping the wrist loose but changing bow direction with the fingers, they found the right hand and the forearm more relaxed while the sound was less stiff. Piatigorsky tried it himself and made adjustments for his students.

The class was allowed to attend the Sunday morning dress rehearsals for the Berlin Philharmonic. Furtwangler was the principal conductor, but there were also guest conductors and soloists: "You could hear everybody under the sun, from Heifetz to Meyer-Mahr." Furtwängler had an unusual motion while conducting—as Lev put it, "almost painting the air"—and his cello section was famous throughout the world. Sometimes students were permitted in the general rehearsals as apprentices. Furtwangler required the highest performance from the moment of tuning, "very refined use of the strings, hearing the fifths perfectly in tune and vibrato linked to the bowing arm. . . . He was fanatically involved in this kind of thinking."

At the Hochschule für Musik, Lev took classes with Franz Schreker, Josef Wolfsthal, and Paul Hindemith. Later he liked to tell the story of an evening of chamber music at Hindemith's flat when Artur Schnabel and Albert Einstein were guests. The physicist, taking the second violin part, was persistently out of tune, misreading notes, and losing tempo, and Schnabel asked him, "Can't you count to four?"

With three German friends from the Hochschule, Lev formed a quartet called Peters, named for the first violinist. They earned money with movie house orchestras, and between shows they performed chamber music, changing programs every night. Their audience was "the other musicians, ushers, cigarette girls, and cleaning women." Once they were hired to play at the Gloria Palace on Kurfurstendamn in an orchestra of sixty musicians conducted by the composer Giuseppe Becce. The last movie they did was *La Bohème* with Lillian Gish, who had come from America with her sister Dorothy. The movie stars created a traffic jam on opening night. Not long after that, recorded sound put them out of the movie business.

Chapter 4

Amati

> *Occupation: Musician.*
> *If I've learned one thing in my life it's: Respect your fellow man.*
>
> *My friends like me because: I like them and I like to tell stories.*
>
> *My mother's best advice was: Practice the cello and marry a beautiful girl. . . . I followed that advice.*
>
> *My mother's worst advice: She never gave me bad advice.*
>
> *When I'm nervous I: Use my common sense to try to see things clearly.*
>
> *I never could: Marry for money . . .*
>
> *The guests at my fantasy dinner party would be: Beethoven, Catherine the Great, Michelangelo, Lucrezia Borgia . . .*
>
> *Most valued material possession? My cello and two bows given me by my teacher.*

The luthier Nicolò Amati may have made twenty cellos in his lifetime. Thirteen or fourteen may have survived.

Most of the catalogued ones are owned by conservatories, museums, and prominent dealers. They're used by virtuosos. Nicolò was the grandson of Andrea Amati, patriarch of the Cremonese school of violin makers and one of the inventors of the modern cello with its enlarged proportions. Historians note that Nicolò lived through the war and famine of 1628, followed by the bubonic plague, which had already struck Northern Europe. He must have witnessed terrible sights: streets banked with mounds of rotting corpses surrounded by bandages and blood-soaked straw, the black-robed *monatti*—the corpse carriers—leading horse carts piled high with putrefying bodies. More than 17,000 of Cremona's population of 37,000 died in the plague. Nicolò's mother and father, two sisters, and a brother-in-law perished. Alessandro Manzoni wrote about it this way: "They're awful things— things we never thought to see; things to prevent one's being happy again for the rest of one's life.... "

Miraculously, Nicolò survived, and he became the preeminent luthier in Italy, known for his beautiful craftsmanship, classical bending lines, the wide gooseneck *f* holes, the balanced, golden curve of the volute, and the rounded scroll, as well proportioned as the torso of a Renaissance sculpture. Among his clients was the French royal court. Though they weren't constructed with the goal of filling large performance halls, his instruments were crafted with profound acoustic understanding. Experts say the Amati approaches the sound of the flute in tone.

Cremonese violins, violas, cellos, and basses have changed hands for four centuries, passing to wives or husbands, children, pupils, friends, creditors, and sometimes strangers. In times of war and upheaval they've been stored in cellars, garrets, barns, and churches. Many were salvaged by "the violin hunter," Luigi Tarisio, who bargained for them in Italy before carrying them to Paris, where they were sold and restored. Like other objects, they crossed borders and were stolen, sold, traded, warehoused, auctioned, bartered, hidden, given away, exchanged as bribes, shot by bullets, thrown out of windows, stored under beds and in closets, transported, carted, buried (like the vessels observant Jews purify), burned, swept out to sea, strapped to men's shoulders. Owners could be secretive about instruments for any number of reasons, and provenance of fine stringed instruments—the history of ownership based upon inventories, catalogues, records of sale and repair—has almost always been anecdotal and incomplete. Dealers don't always keep full record on their file certificates and sale books are not open to the public.

During the 1930s and 1940s, a large number of musical instruments changed hands in Europe, as the situation deteriorated in Germany and the Reich countries. Some were sold by owners who were desperate for cash—musicians or collectors who were emigrating and others who were staying behind but had lost their source of income. Sometimes instruments were simply abandoned by people who were arrested, beaten by vigilantes, or murdered. Other times, they were placed with neighbors or business partners for safekeeping. Instruments, like other household goods, were confiscated from sealed apartments by authorities, local police or administrators, German officials, or army officers. Sometimes, by default, they became the property of the apartment's next tenant.

Throughout the war, most of the great instruments remained in the hands of their eminent owners. (As one violin maker put it, "Great musicians usually have long relationships with their instruments. There is no line between the player and the instrument—many instruments survived the war years because of this. They were protected.") A significant number were taken into the possession of Alfred Rosenberg's special task force for music, Sonderstab Musik, made up of Nazi specialists, connoisseurs, and musicologists who conducted searches of libraries, museums, and Jewish households, confiscating precious instruments. Some of the booty arrived at collection points with meticulous records on note cards. Much of it was shipped east, stolen a second time— sometimes off the trains, destroyed by bombs, or perhaps buried in salt mines that have yet to be uncovered. Lesser instruments were warehoused—hung on closet bars in storage spaces—varnished, silent, wooden boxes. After the war, like everything else, instruments got into the hands of smugglers or were dumped in the warehouses of "liberated" objects. Occasionally a well-known instrument might find its way to a knowledgeable dealer. This was the case with a stolen Stradivarius that Matthias Niessen recognized and returned to its rightful owner—Piatigorsky in 1954.

In a letter dated September 22, 1948, Lev wrote to the philanthropist William Rosenwald: "Before the war started, I had a wonderful Amati cello. . . ." We can only speculate about the source of the "wonderful" instrument that came into Lev's possession in the 1930s, most likely in 1932 or 1933 when he had finished lessons in Berlin. Zorach Aronson might have financed the purchase with furs from his inventory—sable skins were particularly sought after in the unstable world economy. It's possible that Piatigorsky acquired the cello and two bows and lent them to Lev, or he could have located a patron. The Jewish banker Wilhelm Kux had loaned a Nicolò Amati cello to Emanuel Feuerman when he was studying with Julius Klengel in Leipzig. In recitals, Lev had a range of repertoire but often played the sonatas by Locatelli, Eccles, and Vivaldi as well as Couperin's *Siciliana*—music that would have been a particularly effective match for the Amati with its sweet resonance and pure overtones. With its "beautifully floating tone," the magnificent instrument would fit Lev's particular gift and boost the young cellist's chance to launch a solo career.

Can we even be sure it was an Amati? At best we can assume the cello must have been close to museum quality, since less valuable instruments were not confiscated during the first week of occupation—some remaining with their owners long enough to be carried from apartments and houses into the Riga Ghetto. I asked Carla Shapreau, a specialist in musical cultural property of the Nazi era and post-war period, how authenticity of stringed instruments was established in the 1930s. Here is her answer: "Then as now, expertise arose from years of analysis, through examination of many instruments of the violin family. Detailed documentation, including notes, measurements, and photographs, was often obtained for reference and study. Access to old works was essential to develop this expertise, as was a talented eye. Provenance for any given instrument also would have played a significant role in determining authenticity." Connoisseurs, violin makers, and scholars analyze an instrument inside and out. It's possible—and customary—to entirely disassemble a cello that needs repair, inserting a knife into the seams, separating the neck from the sound box and the belly from the ribs. In this way, a luthier becomes familiar with the instrument's anatomy, observing notches and tool marks left in the mold, lining, frame, and purfling; memorizing the signature carving of the head and peg box, the arching and edging, and the shape of the *f* holes; noticing repairs, patterns in the wood grain, and chips in the varnish. Every master leaves his "fingerprints" in dozens of different places. In Berlin, Lev would have had access to the expertise of the leading local dealers, Hammig and Emil Herrmann, or Hamma in Stuttgard, whose certificates of authenticity would be taken into account today.

It is not clear whether Lev's cellos and bows fell into the hands of Alfred Rosenberg's Sonderstab Musik and were therefore shipped to Berlin, whether they were stolen by one of the local German officials who kept Latvian Jewish property for themselves, or whether they remained with the principal cellist of the Radio Orchestra.

Riga had had many warehouses with the property of the liquidated Jews. One of the witnesses, Richard Dannler, who worked as an SS mail carrier under Friedrich Jeckeln, testified at Nuremberg: "I saw boxes full of silver, gold, and diamonds. Currency and bank notes were sorted into bundles and sent to the Deutsche Handelsbank in Riga. There were large amounts of diamonds, jewelry, and gold watches. Jeckeln selected out the best pieces for himself. Sometimes when I would bring him the mail I'd notice various precious objects lying on his desk." If the Amati remained with the cellist, Lev's old colleague, it would have been evacuated in September 1944 with the Radio Orchestra, departing at just about the same time the surviving Jewish prisoners were transported from Riga harbor.

After the war, the governments that housed archives with information about the fate of Europe's stolen goods were not forthcoming and Lev no longer had personal documents from Riga. Most photographs, insurance records, bills of sale, and paperwork had been destroyed. Although he knew the whereabouts of his old colleague from the Radio Orchestra and once in a while talked about going to see him, he shrugged it off, "What's the use?"

1932

PARIS

After graduation, during the summer of 1932, Lev was in Paris. He went to lectures given by Pablo Casals, Jacques Thibaud, and Alfred Cortot at École Normale de

Musique. He lived on rue de la Santé. In the mornings he opened the shutters to his room and looked across to his neighbor's window, where there was always "a pair of crossed hands resting on the ledge." The hands appeared under closed curtains; "the beauty of the long, tapering, symmetrical hands was beyond description." At first he studied them. He smiled to himself and politely turned away, but after several days he was determined to see the face that belonged to the beautiful hands and decided to remain at his post for as long as it would take. One morning he stayed there, waiting until he thought he could no longer bear the tension. That was when the drapery covering the window was drawn aside and an old woman leaned across, lifting up the hands and arranging another set in their place. The hag was the maker of hands and arms displayed in shop windows.

Lev stored away the grotesque illusion. In Paris he fell in love with Eugenia—Genya—who had a heart-shaped face and Claudette Colbert's mysterious smile, "the best . . . the most generous, the most beautiful woman in my entire life . . . and when she died life almost stopped."

1932–33
BERLIN

Lev returned to Berlin to perform with Peters. Perhaps, also, to make preparations for a music competition he hoped would establish his performance credentials. Planning ahead, he wanted to follow his mentor Piatigorsky, carving a career as a soloist. He had already performed a summer concert in Jurmala with the conductor Lovro von Matačić and had expectations for himself and the cello.

Berlin had changed considerably, and Lev was startled by what he saw. During the summer, paramilitary had incited riots and a free-for-all at the university. Now violence and disruptive strikes were common in the streets. The mordant joke was going around: "Brownshirts? You know the Spartans wore red cloaks into battle so the enemy wouldn't see them bleed—the Nazis, they're wearing brown pants so no one will see them . . ."

With dark blond hair and blue eyes, Lev didn't stand out as a Jew. At first he thought he could weather the storm. To stay clear of provocateurs, he began to go by the Latvian "Arnovs" or Russian "Arnoff," honoring his mother's relative who had introduced him to the cello. Just after Hitler became chancellor, Peters gave a performance that Göring attended. It was a close call. To avoid future harassment, they began to entertain in smaller cities in the outskirts of Germany and Belgium— "Every small town had a soft spot for chamber music and a concert series." When one of their members dropped out, they tried to continue as a trio but the campaign against foreigners was relentless, and streets were crowded with military bands, children marching with flags, women reading tracts, and sullen young men looking for fights. In February the Reichstag was set on fire. Lev was deeply affected by the ghostly image of the enormous structure entirely illuminated by flames, smoke pouring from the spout of its giant glass-and-steel dome. Reluctantly he made plans to leave the city.

MAY 1933

MOSCOW

The last round of the All-Union Music Competition of Young Performers began in Moscow on May 10, 1933. At the close, the judges awarded twenty-six prizes in different categories, but the stars were the piano prodigy from Odessa, Emil Gilels, and the cellist Svyatoslav Knushevitsky, an astonishing young musician who was already principal in the Bolshoi Orchestra. In Dallas, decades later, surrounded by students who revered him, Lev talked about attending a competition and winning a prize in Moscow. Perhaps he qualified because of his years in Voronezh. In his notes he wrote, "I met the wonderful cellist Knushevitsky, Malkovsky, and the conductor Golovanov." The award, he explained, consisted of a small amount of money and the opportunity for "permanent residency in Moscow," which he happily declined. The prize, he said, fortified him to go on with the cello.

SUMMER 1933

RIGA

Lev returned to Riga, where he was surrounded by his family and childhood friends. When the weather turned warm, everyone took trains to Jurmala—to the beach with its white quartz sand, Victorian wood-frame hotels, fresh springs, mud baths, casinos, and band shells. That was where Lev met Vladimir Shavitch, the flamboyant guest conductor for the Latvian National Opera Orchestra. Shavitch, a brilliant musician and concocter of schemes, had once been a student of Busoni and Leopold Godowski.

He was a startling presence: long, dark, leathery face made even narrower with sideburns and burning, deep-set eyes. He wore crisp, pleated shirts and dotted bow ties, and there was always a cigarette dangling in his yellowed fingers. Shavitch had lived in South America, Berlin, and New York and had conducted in Moscow, San Francisco, Montevideo, Rochester, Syracuse, Paris, and London. Currently he was promoting "Synchro-Opera"—the idea that by combining movies that were now made with a soundtrack and live opera he could "reduce opera's excess baggage." In the festive summer atmosphere Shavitch and Lev became friends. He listened to Lev play the cello and was impressed with the young man and the golden tone of his instrument. Warning him not to get stuck in Latvia, a small country with limited chance for advancement, he invited Lev to join him in Florence, "his next stop in Europe."

AUTUMN 1933
FLORENCE

Lev was inspired by Shavitch's praise and, with the hope that the conductor could help him launch his career, he set off for Italy. Shavitch met him at the station at Santa Maria Novella and they walked together, cello on Lev's shoulder, to the Arno and over Ponte Santa Trinità to Lungarno Guicciardini 19, the home of an American patroness of the arts, a millionaire from New York, Mrs. Daliba Jones. Mrs. Jones lived in a palazzo built and furnished in the grand style with crystal chandeliers, gilded clocks, porcelain urns, and marquetry cabinets.

Lev was exhausted that evening, but after dinner he played chamber music, Beethoven's C minor Trio and Tchaikovsky's A minor Trio with the elegiac themes that later would become famous among the Riga Jews. He played with a young violinist who was also from out of town and with Shavitch's wife, Tina Lerner, a concert pianist known for her interpretation of the Romantic repertoire. The mood of the Tchaikovsky Trio, both lyrical and introspective, must have drawn Lev's thoughts to Genya, to Berlin, and back to Riga, to his parents and perhaps the tragedies in their early lives. When they finished playing, Mrs. Daliba Jones stuffed an envelope with fifty dollars into Lev's music. She repeated this whenever Lev played in her house and encouraged Shavitch to promote his young friend. With their help Lev was invited to perform at the Latvian embassy in Rome, and Shavitch introduced him to his booking agent, Franco Parcilli. This was the beginning of a series of concerts Lev gave in Italy, Spain, France, and Belgium. In London he played for BBC Radio and was paid "a pound a minute." The response to his tour was good, critics praising the cellist and his Amati: "sound of his instrumental singing . . ." "light, floating cello tone . . ." "tone is sweet . . ."

GENYA

I have three photographs of Genya with Lev. The first: at the seashore—drift nets and herring boats, makeshift beach houses in the background, a handsome middle-

aged couple, a man in robe, then Genya and Lev dressed
for the city. Genya, her hat tilted to the side, is graceful
and self-possessed. There's little doubt she was one of the
"beauties in exile"—émigrées who lived in Paris, Berlin,
or Constantinople and worked in the world of fashion
for the Russian houses of couture and later in film. In
the second picture, dated "Florence, October 1933,"
she and Lev are standing against a balustrade on Piazzale
Michelangelo. The domes, towers, and sloping hills
of Florence lie behind them. Wearing a flowing gown,
flower in the buttonhole of her jacket, beret tipped to
the side, Genya gazes into the camera with a mysterious
half-smile. The third photograph is dated "Paris, January
1934." Lev's taken off his hat and wrapped his arm
around his beautiful friend. Again, she is splendidly
dressed, this time in a winter coat with fur collar and
cuffs. Her hands are large and plump. The back of the
photograph reads in English: "To *Dallinotschica*, With
all my love. Lyova."

LENINGRAD
1935

If it's true that Lev was in Moscow for the music
competition, he would have been aware of the harsh
circumstances for those living in the Soviet Union at the
time. Nonetheless, two years later, in 1935, he was in
Leningrad, auditioning for the principal cellist's chair
with the Leningrad Philharmonic under Fritz Stiedry.
He made an impression as a "young swaggering fellow,"

according to the assistant conductor, Daniel Sternberg, who recommended him for the job. Sternberg said, "I think we could do no better than to hire this man." But a Jew born in Germany, who had lived in Riga, Berlin, and Florence, posed too many problems. Lev was not given the position, and soon he returned home. Now, in order to retain his passport, it was time to fulfill his military service. To his delight, the requirement wasn't strenuous. An old school friend and pianist, the son of the president of Latvia, was also doing service. Together, they played Beethoven duets, sometimes joined by the pianist Victor Babin. Each week they presented paperwork to the military and the government rubber-stamped it.

RIGA AND ABROAD

Even at home it was not easy to establish a place in the music community, where openings customarily would be offered first to Latvian musicians with Christian backgrounds. Lev gave some recitals at the conservatory, performing with the accompanists Herman Braun and Mira Hazan. At Melngalvju nams he performed with Peter Schubert. They played works by Eccles and Haydn, a Chopin sonata, Piatigorsky's adaptation of *Nocturne* by Ravel, the *Nigun* from Bloch's *Baal Shem (Three Pictures of Chassidic Life)*, and Cassadó's *Requiebros*. He made four recordings with the pianist Leo Dimant on the Latvian label, Bellaccord Electro. He took courses at the conservatory and got bookings to tour Scandinavia with some of the celebrities who hadn't yet emigrated:

the beautiful young dancer Mia Slavenska, who won the 1936 Dance Olympics, and the charismatic tenor Joseph Schmidt. In the summer of 1937 Lev became the principal cellist in the summer Orchestra of Libau and performed *Handel-Halvorsen Passacaglia* with Karl Westen, first violinist of the Latvian Opera Orchestra. The beloved showpiece provided an opportunity for both men to demonstrate technical pyrotechnics, speaking with their bows, matching tone and tempi, adjusting to one another within the structure of the Baroque pattern. Through the music they became intertwined. Four years later Westen risked his life on Lev's behalf.

Chapter 5

On the Verge of War

SPRING AND SUMMER 1938

RIGA

The political situation in Latvia was unraveling. Karl
Ulmanis ruled by fiat, and it was part of his agenda to
diminish the influence of Jewish and German minorities.
While there had always been anti-Semitism, now the
Jewish community was more stigmatized and isolated.
The conductor Paul Breisach invited Lev to perform
Bloch's *Schelomo* with the Libau orchestra, but in the
summer of 1938 the orchestra trustees wouldn't allow
a Jewish musician to play Jewish music on their stage.
Still, as Daniel Sternberg put it, Riga was a place where
many artists and intellectuals "felt safe . . . a city of some
culture and some distinction. . . ." Lev continued to feel
he would weather the storm; this wasn't the backwater of
his early childhood. He remained busy, playing chamber
music, studying scores, and arranging recitals. He had
the Amati, which connected him to the broader world.

AUTUMN 1938

RIGA

By the autumn of 1938, it had become almost impossible to make a living. The state-supported orchestras were not hiring Jews, and it was equally hard to obtain a teaching position. Latvian music students were choosing Latvian teachers who could promote them. In the conservatory there were hardly any Jewish students because their families were struggling just to survive and looking for ways to emigrate. Nonetheless, two Jewish boys came to Lev asking for lessons. At first he thought "they were absolutely unmusical, musically deaf"; they simply wanted distraction from the hardships their families were enduring. The boys were too poor to pay for instruction, but Lev found a set of student cellos and agreed to teach them as "an escape from his situation" and a challenge: "I had to help them but didn't know how. Gradually, I began to discover the how and why of these problems and built up my own ideas about cello playing...." Over a few months, the boys made enough progress to give a recital, and soon they were referring to themselves as cellists.

Other people began asking for lessons. A woman came to him with a unique problem: "My older son plays the violin. He's played for some time. The other boy's been handicapped since birth. He doesn't have fingers on his right hand, and the fingers on his left hand are deformed. It breaks my heart to see the little boy listening to his brother and wanting to make music himself. I can read in his eyes the misery that's in his heart."

Lev asked her to bring the boy to his apartment; he'd talk to him and see what could be done.

The child was nine years old. He had a beautiful smile and large, dark brown eyes, but he was small and fragile. When Lev shook his hand it felt strangely like a paw. He looked at the boy, and the child shifted his gaze in shame, quickly withdrawing his little hand from the handshake. Lev asked him to come back in a few days.

When the boy left, Lev couldn't find peace with himself. What could he do to help the child? Many thoughts raced through his mind. Finally, he decided to construct a special adjustment for the frog of the bow. The frog, "the nut of the bow," is U-shaped and often made of ebony, fastening to the bow hair on one side and fitting against the bow stick on the other. It's usually just large enough to allow space for the side of the tip of the thumb to rest inside.

Lev needed to adapt the frog to the shape of the boy's hand. His first idea was to build a handle from clay, placing it over the frog "like a saddle." He put a hole through it as a grip for the "paw" to rest on. Luckily the boy had a thumb that could be placed in the right spot on the frog. In that way he would have a hold on the bow. But after a day, the clay became hard as stone and cracked. Lev decided to replace it with cork.

Lev brought the bow to the child's house to see if it would work. The boy slipped his hand through the "handle," and it fit. With this success he obtained another small cello and began lessons. The boy took his studies seriously and developed a lovely sound and was able to learn many small pieces.

Another student, named Bavinka Neuhaus, appeared at Lev's door. He was eight years old and had an extraordinary talent. Within a year and a half he could play the passionate first Saint-Saëns concerto with expertise. He had a marvelous memory and could compose his own pieces. He was joined by one more child, Eugene Perevosky, who also had a real talent. Eugene and Bavinka played the Handel Sonata for two cellos. Eventually Lev added an older student, a man who had once been a director for Twentieth Century Fox and now wanted to learn the cello. His name was Gus Geoffey. Sometimes Gus played while Bavinka sat on Lev's lap. The boy would correct the man's mistakes, demonstrating phrasing and the runs in difficult passages. In Riga, Bavinka became known as "the little Mozart."

1939

PARIS

Genya wrote to Lev with terrible news. The doctors said she had cancer and "must undergo a dreadful operation." Surgery and radium treatments were arranged. In the spring of 1939 Lev went to Paris to be with his old friend and help her family.

Genya lingered for many weeks, but there was little hope in the wards of the French hospital. Lev spent most of his time at her bedside, but one day for distraction he decided to go to a music shop. He followed Boulevard Haussmann to Café de l'Opéra. He noticed the plane trees, shimmering and fragrant. He walked on toward Durand's music store, trying to rid himself of oppressive thoughts. When he was about to enter the shop, to his amazement, he saw his old teacher standing in the door in front of him. Piatigorsky had remarried and was in Paris with his new wife and their infant daughter. Lev told him about Eugenia, and Piatigorsky was grieved to hear about the beautiful young woman and concerned about his friend. He invited Lev to the home of his father-in-law, the banker Baron Edouard de Rothschild.

The Rothschild family lived in a mansion on the outskirts of the city, as Lev put it, "a castle that even had a chapel with religious artifacts, including one of the most ancient torahs." Conversation at dinner was dominated by the subject of war. Would Germany and Russia partition Poland? Would Hitler attack in September? Would he stage a pogrom with the first act of war? The baron, with "great flair," asked Lev about his plans and warned him not to return to Riga. "No Jew," he said sharply, "should remain in Europe. If you go back to Latvia it may well be too late." The baron said he would help Lev emigrate or at least he could stay with the Rothschild family in Paris as a guest. It was a generous offer, and Lev thought about it often in the years to come.

1939

BERLIN

After Genya's death, Lev packed his bags and, with his cello, boarded a train, "a strange feeling in his heart." The tragedy disoriented him. He had haphazard plans to renegotiate the contract he had signed with the Libau orchestra. His parents and sister were still in Riga. Perhaps he could convince his family to come to Paris.

On his way to Berlin he was overwhelmed by memories of his student years and a feeling of loss for Genya and his own youthful ambitions. Most of his friends had left Germany. In his thoughts, he made a list of musicians he had encountered in Berlin: Furtwängler, Casals, Fritz Kreisler, Rosenthal, Ossip Gabrilowitsch, Mischa Elman, Feuermann, Schnable, Carl Flesch, Lotte Lehman, Bruno Walter, Klemperer, Erich Kleiber, Vladimir Horowitz, Milstein. The names went on. Berlin was entirely different now. Professional musicians and amateurs had been "squeezed out" after the anti-Jewish boycotts in 1933, the graffiti—*Dreckjude-Talmud Gaunef*—the beatings and arrests, the purge of Jewish musicians from German orchestras and stages, and the publication of *Lexikon der Juden in der Musik*. Jewish friends performed in the Kulturbund Orchestra, but their lives were a torment of uncertainty, isolation, fear, and humiliation.

There were hundreds of stories. Lev may have heard how unemployed Jews had become middlemen, arranging sales of string instruments belonging to those who were down on their luck, imprisoned, or victims of extortionists. There was also the story of Hans Bottermund, a "half-Jew," born in Leipzig. Before the war, Bottermund sat in Piatigorsky's chair as principal cellist and soloist with the Berlin Philharmonic. During the Hitler years, he was one of a handful of musicians whom Wilhelm Furtwängler tried to protect. He and his Danish wife had permission to remain in Germany through the Nazi years, although they lived in poverty. In 1938 Bottermund brought his cello, a Guarnerius built in 1694, to Copenhagen, placed it in a bank vault, and inserted the following into the cello case:

Copenhagen, September, 1938
To the Unknown Future Owner of my Guarnerius
Cello:

Dear Sir,
I don't know whether you're a professional cellist or
an amateur. I don't know which country you're from,
which nation or religion you belong to, but it might be
interesting for you to know about the former owners of
the instrument. In any case, I was always interested
in such things and was able to find, starting from
c. 1780, the following information: The farthest back
owner that I know of was a cleric whose name was
"Fendt." He lived in Balzano. Around 1814, the cello
was sold for 100 golddulkaten in Prague to a man
named Gens-Bacher. After that, the solo cellist of the
Dresden Hof Opera, Hofrat Böckmann, purchased it
(he was in Dresden at the same time as Guitzmacher).
I obtained the cello from Böckmann (it was given to
me as a gift by some patrons of music).

I have played the instrument in all my concerts
since 1912. Only occasionally during the world war, I
kept it in a safe. I write these lines in a very depressed
sate of mind. Circumstances that are against me (I
am half-Jewish) force me to take my cello out of the
country—this wonderful cello, the most beautiful
cello I've played in my whole life. The Hitler regime

does not allow me to concertize. The sale of my records (which I played on the Guarnerius) is forbidden in Germany.

Any day I might lose my position as principal cellist at the Berlin Philharmonic. Only the Director, Furtwängler, has been able to get permission for me to stay in the orchestra on a day by day basis.

Hans Bottermund

After writing the first letter, Mr. Bottermund wrote a second letter which was also placed inside the cello case:

Copenhagen, 1938
Letter to the Owner of My Guarnerius Cello:

Concern for the future of my cello caused me to take my cello to Copenhagen where it is in a safe.

Now I cannot play anymore on my instrument, the wonderful cello, my dear comrade for twenty-five years.

I remember when I had my twenty-first birthday and I chanced to play in a symphony concert at the Dresden Opera House. At that event I tried out the cello. Four days before, I had played a Montagna from Hamma, owned by Hill of London. Also, there was a Strad from Caressa that happened to be in Dresden. Of all the master cellos, I chose this Guarnerius—I never regretted it. I have never heard a more triumphant, bright, yet round, big tone on all four strings. I have never known a cello with such a D string—that in spite of the comparatively small measurement of the instrument in length. The strings are so strong, even with the greatest strength, one cannot overplay this cello. Maybe I will never again hear this sound—I know every little nuance so well. All other instruments which I'll play later in life will always arouse in me my desire to play my Guarnerius.

Out of great concern for the safety of my wife and the continuation of our life ahead, I take this absurd step which robs me and hinders me from playing my cello.

Hans Bottermund

Half a century later, John Sharp—principal cellist in the Chicago Symphony and an old student of Lev Aronson's—purchased Bottermund's instrument with the "triumphant, bright, yet round, big tone," and the two letters that had been stored in its case.

RETURNING HOME

Lev was haunted by what he heard and saw in Berlin. He had remembered the city as a Mecca, but that was over. With the Amati on his shoulder, he boarded a train to Riga and then Jurmala. It was a relief to return to the warm circle of affection—parents, sister, aunt, uncle—a small table with a white cloth set out in the sea air, plates of herring salad, and wild strawberries. "And why have you come back to this future inferno?" his childhood friend Benya Levitas asked.

1940
RIGA

The Soviet annexation of Latvia began in the summer of 1940 and lasted for what Latvians call *Baigais gads*, "the horrible year." Businesses and houses, especially those in the countryside, were confiscated and nationalized. People were arrested by the military and tortured, others were shot execution-style in the back of the head. In June 1941, just before the German invasion, more than 15,000 people, property owners, members of the middle class, local politicians, and intellectuals—about a third of them Jewish—were evacuated in sealed boxcars, and most of them were sent to the gulag.

For Latvians, the loss of national sovereignty was infuriating, but for Jewish musicians and performers the Sovietization was a mixed blessing. Once again they were allowed to perform on stage. There were no banks under the Soviets, but Lev was paid well enough that the money box in his cabinet drawer was filled. He was close to achieving his goal of becoming a famous musician; his recordings on the Amati were broadcast on radio.

Leo Blech, who had led the Berlin State Opera until 1937, was the conductor of the Latvian SSR State Opera and Ballet Theatre. Working with him was an education in itself. Lev described his audition in an interview for the *Strad*: "[Leo Blech] once asked me to go to the library and select music for a cello audition. Since I was very young, I chose the most difficult passages in the repertoire, excerpts from *Rheingold*, *Tristan*, and *Parsifal*, etc. and with great pride returned and placed them on his desk. He looked them over and then said, 'Tell me, what is the purpose of this audition? Is it that we wish to discover what someone *can* play or what he *cannot*? I want to hear how he plays the solo in the *William Tell* Overture or how his vibrato distributes in the *Swan*.'"

The sphere of Lev's professional activities was now expanded. His friends included Osvalds Lēmanis, choreographer and director of the ballet, the world-famous tenor Mariss Vetra, and the Wagnerian diva Paula Brivkalne. He sat in cafés with the publisher Helmar Rudzitis, as he put it, "talking for hours, solving the problems of the world." With his earnings, he was able to take an apartment in the beautiful art deco building at 25 Jauniela, the façade ornamented with Jugendstil masks, gargoyles, and winding grapevines. He continued to teach his students. And so he remained in Riga with the Amati.

22 JUNE 1941
RIGA

Everyone was surprised, but life continued ...

Over the weekend, diplomatic cars had been going from the beach to the city, their license plates "black on white, bearing the letters: C.D." Now at the morning rehearsal of the Libau orchestra, Lev noticed the doorman was away from his post. The locker rooms, usually full of commotion preceding rehearsal, were half-empty. Thirty minutes before rehearsal, a musician cried out: "There's war!" A meeting of orchestra administrators was called, and not long after that everyone heard sounds of the first air raid and the wail of sirens. When rehearsal began the mood had been transformed in an instant. Everyone felt the change and a new uncertainty.

Two days later, from the bridges of the Daugava River, Lev watched an endless line of Russian armored cars and trucks with soldiers. Then "with the roar of tanks, cannons, Stukas that not only woke the people but woke the earth itself," the German army invaded and there was barely resistance. With guns and bayonets from 1914, the Soviets were no match against the modern German army. Their canons dragged by six or eight field horses were museum pieces. Messerschmitts bombarded Riga and snipers, collaborators, members of the paramilitary *Aizsargi* and *Perkonkrusts* shot at the Russians from the windows and roofs. On the ground, local children were drafted as "cannon futter" and killed in the first wave of fighting. Hundreds of little bodies lay by the bridge in a heap of blood and mud. After that, in battle, some of the German soldiers advanced with gun barrels down. The Russian soldiers were routed. They came through the city, "in an absolutely chaotic condition. Their shoes were ragged, their clothes were torn. They had abandoned their rifles." They came in broken-down divisions, dragging through, begging anyone for food, bread, and water. The Latvians were bitter and threw water on them.

Fifteen hours after Germany declared war against the Soviet Union, Radio Kaunas had begun running its broadcasts in German. On the streets or in the orchestra hall, suddenly everyone was speaking in broken German. Lev walked with the Amati on the sidewalks and everyone he passed was carrying German books.

Chapter 6

Without an Instrument

29 JUNE 1941

RIGA

During the bombardment on the left bank of the Daugava River, Lev and his family found shelter with neighbors in the cellar of their tall apartment building. The cellar, which had been used for storing coal, was now crowded with people from different nationalities and walks of life: a Latvian lawyer and his wife, a German family with three small children, the aristocratic widow of a White Russian, "Malka the whore," a Chinese wrestler "who was caught in the blitz attack while performing in the Riga circus." Lev remembered a guttering candle that emitted enough of "an eerie orange-blue glow" to illuminate the group crouching together and trying to comfort one another, arms wrapped around shoulders or waists.

Artillery could be heard from across the river and then coming closer, rattling other buildings in the neighborhood, causing windows to shatter. An odd silence followed before they heard a huge explosion. A shell hit their building. Walls shook. Stones and debris fell from the ceiling, and a portion of the central structure collapsed.

Now in the basement, they were cut off. The concierge who was with them in the cellar yelled, "You've got to break through the wall or we'll suffocate!" The Chinese wrestler grabbed one of the ice axes kept in the basement for breaking frozen snow in the winter and began chopping against the wall. Others joined him, jabbing at the plaster with long steel rods. Soon there was similar hammering on the other side, and they could hear the voice of their *dvornik*, the porter, calling out.

Finally they made a hole. The wrestler and a lawyer who was one of the tenants helped the others squeeze through. When they were safely out on a back street, Lev heard a groaning coming from where they'd been trapped. He and his father turned back and found the Chinese wrestler, too large to escape through the hole: "half his body was out and half his body was in." They pulled and chopped at the rock and pushed until finally he was free. Crying in gratitude, the wrestler wrapped his huge arms around his new friends. His name was Chiutan.

While parts of the old city were still burning, the Aronson family and Chiutan followed miles of empty streets until they reached safety in another section of town. Lev had Russian money in his pocket, and he used it as a bribe to get into a shelter. The Latvians in charge didn't want to allow the wrestler. They said German authorities would object to a Chinese refuge. Zorach intervened: "Don't you see, he's *Japanese* and an ally?"

The shelter was set up with rows of beds made out of planks, and the exhausted friends settled down for the night. While he was half-asleep, Lev overheard two men planning to kill them with daggers. Then, "Not now! Wait!" one said to the other. "Wait till the Germans get here."

In the morning, the Aronsons left quickly, making their way to the close quarters of Lev's three-room apartment. That's where they remained, the five of them, since Chiutan was now considered part of the family.

For several days, anticipating the German occupation, they didn't venture outside. Christian friends from the music world brought "food, drink, cigarettes . . . a bottle of vodka to keep us going." Lev's mother took her leather and chamois-lined bag of jewelry—"rings, necklaces, brooches, the gold watch she wore on a chain"—and gave it to the opera singer Paula Brivkalne, who promised to hold it until the time when it would be needed for barter and bribes.

Finally, the knock at the door, two Latvians wearing armbands, one holding a document: "Are you the cellist? You have two cellos, four bows, and cases. Get your instruments. Follow us."

7 JULY 1941

RIGA

Later in life, when he returned to the story of the confiscation of his instruments, the elements were always the same: the knock on the door, two Latvians wearing armbands, mounting the cement steps of the central post office, his colleague's averted glance, laughter, a hand on his coat collar, a kick or a push, falling, tumbling down the shaft of the stairwell.

Opposite the post office there was a park with benches. Lev crossed the road in a daze. His trousers were ripped, his cheek and the bridge of his nose were bleeding. He sat in the half-shade under a broad oak. He thought about the Amati. He felt as though he had "forcibly delivered a friend." After several minutes Lev painfully stood up. There was an odd noise in his ear. Since childhood this was a sound he had heard whenever there was complete silence. He knew he had to get back to the apartment where his parents, his sister, and Chiutan were waiting. It was dangerous to be seen on the streets. Many prominent Jewish intellectuals and civic leaders had already been rounded up, shot on the pavement, or dragged to *Zentralka*, Central Prison, or the Riga Police Prefecture. Strangely the fear of being arrested bothered Lev less than the humiliation he had felt among the musicians from the Radio Orchestra.

WITH DEAD EXPRESSIONS

On his way home, Lev passed the Opera House. A group of singers, dancers, and musicians, many old friends and colleagues, were gathered at the stage door. From a distance they seemed to be talking lightheartedly. It felt strange to be without an instrument, but out of habit he approached them anyway. When he came close enough to be noticed, their bodies stiffened, and they looked back at him "with dead expressions." Some turned their gazes and others stepped aside, hurrying into the building. Only the dancer Osvalds Lēmanis moved forward and offered a handshake: "Have faith, old friend. I'll do my best to look out for you." Lev walked on. He understood the need for self-preservation. His relationship to his old colleagues could lead to their interrogation, arrest, or the loss of work. "So why bother?" he asked himself.

Lev's identity as a Jew was now his main concern, and this was a completely new experience. How should he get back to his apartment? He would use the old city's indirect routes, avoiding main thoroughfares and extending time until dusk. In darkness Jews and gentiles appeared the same. The old city was crisscrossed with alleyways and narrow passages connecting the buildings to one another. Houses were so close that neighbors could raise their windows, lean out, and talk; they didn't have to use loud voices. He was able to go a long distance by passing through backyards. Small tunnels and old stone entranceways led to different sections of the old city. The silence was eerie. He could hear the echo of his shoes and an occasional drunkard humming "O Tannenbaum" though it was out of season. Then he was beyond the old city, two-thirds of the way home, past *Pulvertornis*, Gunpowder Tower. He forced himself to walk with confidence, his back straight, his head high, without a trace of meekness. Revelers passed him, their faces flushed from drinking.

8 JULY 1941

RIGA

And so it was odd when they shouted, "Here are your instruments!"

A vehement knock at the door the next morning. Two Latvian collaborators and a German soldier: "All Jewish males will evacuate this building!"

On the street, men gathered from many different apartment buildings, some dressed in summer suits, one with phylacteries on his forehead. They waited for a long time before the strange announcement: "Here are your instruments!" One of the collaborators had buckets, soap, and rags.

Some spectators assembled on the corner as the men were put to work washing the street. A few laughed uncomfortably. Some taunted. The crowd formed a circle and watched as someone was lashed with a leather belt across his naked behind until he was totally covered with blood. The performance continued until people grew bored; even the guards seemed to lose energy. After a while they lined the men up and marched them through the streets.

On their way they encountered Russian prisoners of war, perhaps three hundred of them, in shocking condition. Their hands dangled at their sides and their clothes had been ripped. Some didn't have shoes. Their feet dragged. Lev was amazed to see how expressionless they were, not responding when the Germans struck them with the butts of their guns to make them move forward.

Both groups were ushered through the gates of a city park. The Russians arrived first and they queued up along a series of long, narrow ditches. It looked like a burial ground, and everyone thought the same thing. Several guards pushed the men up to the edge of the ditches.

A uniformed German officer and several Latvians in civilian clothes stepped forward. The German had the soft face of a cleric. It was round and smooth except for the left cheek, which was scarred. He said: "Russian communists tried to destroy the beauty of these parklands, digging trenches for defense against our German army. Their judgment was wrong. Our army won't be stopped by archaic tactics. This is the army of the future, led by the wisdom of the Führer. So that you remember, you'll restore these grounds with bare hands!" The work continued until close to midnight.

9 JULY 1941
RIGA

Lev's hands, so important to the life of a cellist, were being destroyed. The next day he returned to the trenches, digging again without a shovel or gloves. His friend, the Chinese wrestler, Chiutan, had wanted to come along, arguing that he could do the work and save Lev's hands, but both knew it was impossible.

In the early afternoon, when the task of filling the trenches was complete, Lev returned to the apartment block. German and Latvian officials were operating the elevators. Lev took the stairwell, wondering what would happen next. On the landing he saw a guard standing in front of his apartment. The door was taped, sealed with a large purple sticker, and on it were printed the words: CONFISCATED BY SECURITY POLICE. Lev approached: "I live here. It's raining. I need a coat."

The guard answered, "You don't live in this apartment any longer. Where you're going you won't need a coat. Get out!" He pushed him down the stairs, and his body bounced against the railing. On the ground floor, another guard was waiting.

But nobody knew what would happen. Lev found his family and many others crowded into the empty apartment of a neighboring building. People were sitting on the floor or leaning against walls. Lev would think back later, "They already appeared to be mourning the dead."

After several hours, the same SD man who had been stationed at the door of Lev's apartment entered with some Latvians. One of them, named Ansons, had been in school with Lev.

"All men, outside!" it was announced.

When they were boys, Ansons's name had appeared next to Lev's on the roster, and sometimes Lev had helped him—"saved his neck"—when school assignments weren't completed.

"Ansons, help my father—not me—he has a leg injury and walks with a cane," Lev whispered.

Ansons didn't answer.

There was turmoil and crying. Then a second announcement: "Young men, out of here! Old men stay! The rest will be turned over to Latvian authorities." Soldiers separated families that clung to one another. But Lev's father had been spared.

Again, Lev was on the street. About twenty men were lined in rows with Latvian guards stationed at five-foot distances around them. Ansons was in front of Lev, a rifle on his shoulder. Lev began talking to him quietly. "Where are we going? Where are they taking us?" Without turning his head, Ansons whispered, "*Zentralka*. Don't ask anything else. Leave me alone. If you ask again, I'll pretend I don't know you. You're on the way to God knows where, and that will be the end of you. I have to go on living. Don't talk to me; it will only get me in trouble."

They paused before a row of trucks parked on the road leading to the Ministry of Interior. A German officer, "a short man with bowed legs, stiff-necked, big teeth, resembling a monkey," ordered the guards to open the gate, and the prisoners were escorted inside. Terra-cotta pots lined the interior of the courtyard. "Now," he said, "stamp your shoes across every bit of ground, corner to corner and diagonally. Don't miss anything. See the flower pots? You'll get in with your feet and stamp them as well. You'll do it until I tell you to stop."

For about an hour the prisoners followed his commands: "To the end of the lawn, run! Faces to the fence! Reverse! Again to the fence! Go to the flower pots! Crawl on your stomachs!"

While the prisoners were stamping to exhaustion, the officer stood on the side with his soldiers, instructing, "On your bellies, crawl to the gate!" He turned to the soldiers and then to the truck drivers, signaling them to come in since he'd been reassured there weren't mines, grenades, or bombs on the grounds.

But it wasn't over. The officer led them to the Ministry, which had been recently occupied by the Soviets. The place was a jumbled wreck; the Russians had left in chaos. Papers were wadded up and in shreds, strewn under the legs of furniture. Desk drawers had been pulled open and torn apart. Files, roped together in bundles, were heaped on the ground. Trash cans were filled with the ashes of singed documents. Everything was covered in thick dust. The door of an enormous and empty, red safe swung open. Someone had left a half-eaten loaf of bread on a table and a bottle of vodka, DKA, on the floor. A raincoat with a captain's insignia was suspended in the air on a hanger. Stalin's and Lenin's pictures hung askew.

The men were silent. Even the officer seemed stunned by the mess. There were several similar rooms, one leading to another.

"All of this will be put in order. All papers gathered, stacked, carried outside, deposited by the side of the building. After that, you'll begin cleaning. Everything must shine. Even the stoves will be cleaned!"

Someone asked if they could have food before working and the officer began a tirade: "On your feet! I'll show you how German soldiers fought on the battlefield, hungry, thirsty, exhausted. If they survived so will you! Down on your stomachs! Crawl! Faster!"

Lev heard the brief click of a revolver chamber opening followed by a gunshot.

They worked methodically into the night. Every half hour, a sergeant shouted, "Count the minutes left to live!"

Some of the men were praying. Lev's fingers were black and bloody. Music was totally out of his consciousness. Soldiers lined the fence with loaded guns, and one of the Jewish workers, too exhausted to care, ran to them: "Get it over. If life is to be like. . . ." Lev and a few others fainted, but their colleagues lifted them up and held them in place.

When they were released, at midnight, Lev stood still for a moment. He was wearing navy trousers and a blue-and-gray checked jacket. His pants had ripped below the knee. Everything was torn. He paused in the darkness to listen. He examined his swollen and filthy knuckles. How could the Amati, built by the luthier of dukes and princes, have belonged in such hands?

END OF JULY 1941
RIGA

Lev didn't touch a musical instrument. He no longer heard music; he was adapting "from dignity to nothingness." With the others who had been in the work crew at the Ministry of Interior, he reported to the street every morning. They formed a queue and were given identification cards that designated them "Gestapo Jews"—among their own people, *Gestapo Judeu*—so that no other Germans would steal them away or harm them "unless they wanted to deal with the Gestapo."

After cleaning the Ministry of Interior, they were assigned to wash and repair cars, clean apartments, organize offices, dispose of garbage, alter uniforms, and shine shoes. Lev learned quickly how to do all of it since "it wasn't pleasant to work with a swollen eye or with pain from a hit with a whip." At their work places they were allowed a half-hour rest, a piece of bread, and a piece of salami. Most of them ate half of what they received, saving the other portion for their families.

AUGUST 1941
RIGA

Every day brought odd requirements: Jews must register, must pin the *Judenstern*—the yellow star—on the left coat pocket, must wear a large *Judenstern* on their backs, can't attend school, can't practice their professions, can't purchase food from local stores, must walk in groups, "never solo," can't walk on sidewalks. A joke went around: "Before, the streets were for pigs and the sidewalks for people. Now it's vice versa."

Many Riga Jews became "personal servants" to particular Germans. Lev Aronson, once the student of Piatigorsky, worked for Sturmbannführer Kelpsch, who was a Teletype operator, "phenomenally fast."

Occasionally there were fights among the Germans who would say to one another: "These Jews work exclusively for me. Find your own Jews, and if you harm my Jews, I'll beat yours." Lev remembered: "What a mentality, what a sense of 'ownership.' For us it was laughter through tears."

Early one morning Kelpsch sent him on an errand to get shoe polish from another German. While Lev was at the officers' quarters, another man injured his heel and was trailing blood across the cement floor.

Lev was ordered to clean up the blood.

"How should I do it?"

"What? Don't make me laugh. You know what to do with blood. Clean it up or I'll slash your face, and there'll be more blood to get rid of."

Lev turned to a boy who served in the kitchen and mumbled, "I'm just a cellist. . . . I don't know what to do. . . ."

The boy explained to him and Lev "fell to the task," scrubbing the floor with water and bleach.

When he was finished, the German looked at him and said, "You knew all the time. You Jews are liars."

Lev returned to Kelpsch and told him the story.

"What? He should be in charge of his own blood. Have him come to me, here."

Lev took the message from Kelpsch to the second German, who said, "Tell him, go to hell!"

Kelpsch, upon hearing this, muttered, "He should be so lucky!"

JAZZ

A German soldier (SD man and amateur pianist) said to Lev: "Jews have poisoned the world with jazz. They've contaminated music! Sure, they play Beethoven, Mozart, and Haydn, but they misinterpret these geniuses."

"When you say that, do you include Schnabel and Heifetz?"

"Well compare Schnabel to Gieseking performing Beethoven, it's entirely different."

Lev agreed.

"Jews latch on to things without understanding."

"Why are you such an anti-Semite?"

"Before the Great Revolution, I lived in the provinces and could barely make a living. It was a great struggle, but I set aside enough money to buy a suit so I could look for work. I went to a shop owned by a Jewish tailor and gave him all the money I had, planning to come up with the rest when the job was done. But the tailor botched it. His measurements were wrong. He didn't press it. The pants were too short. The collar was crumpled. Do you see?"

"Did you pay him?"

"Of course not!"

RIGA GHETTO

At the end of August came an announcement: The Riga Jews would have to live in Moskauer Vorstadt, the poorest section of the city. A map was posted to show the streets that would enclose the ghetto—Maskavas, Vitebskas, Ebreju, Liksnas, Lauvas, Lazdonas, Liela Kainu, Katolu, Jekabpils, and Lacplesa—mapping out the shape of a bottle on its side.

Within a few days, the Gestapo Jews were called together by SD Officer Heinz Truhe, who had "sharp features, thin lips, red hair"—a man so tall and thin he couldn't fill his uniform. Truhe told them they must choose three men to be in charge of the distribution of ghetto apartments, mostly one-story houses made of bare wood or small workers' apartment rooms with low ceilings, the walls often covered with mildew. Many of the buildings had no gas, heat, or plumbing and the new tenants would find them infested with mice, cockroaches, fleas, and bedbugs. Perhaps because of his reputation as a well-known musician, Lev was selected to be one of the leaders. For his services, the Aronson family was assigned "one of the best places."

The move to the ghetto took two months, many people waiting until the last moment. A caravan of stragglers, they walked with hand carts and luggage, perambulators, whatever small items of furniture could be carried across their shoulders and on their backs. On October 25 the ghetto was sealed, enclosed by a double fence of barbed wire and wooden barrier logs—thick posts—set at the entrance. In all, 29,602 Jews would be living in an area that had accommodated 13,000.

TCHAIKOVSKY PIANO TRIO

At first there was some organization—a hospital, a school, ghetto "stores," and soup kitchens. The Jews who worked were allowed half the rations the Latvians received on the other side of the wall, and that was less than the Germans: 120 grams of bread a day, 25 grams of margarine a week, and once a month 175 grams of horsemeat or spoiled fish. Shipments to the ghetto were unpredictable, and people hid their food from thieves, digging under the floor or cutting patches into the walls. Though it was illegal to carry anything through the gates, there might be some provisions—jellies, for instance—left from the previous tenants. "Things were not yet desperate."

Among the Jews, there were several professional musicians. A few had instruments and even had scores. Perhaps to lift their own spirits or to restore a sense of normality, they got together to read chamber music. One day they discovered a piano without legs, a Bechstein that someone had carried into the ghetto. The musicians decided to prop it on concrete blocks and try it out. To their amazement the piano made a pretty good sound, and they thought with this wonderful instrument they could arrange a recital in the hall of the ghetto school. A few days later, the pianist Herman Godes, the violinist Professor Adolf Metz (who had studied with Leopold Auer in St. Petersburg and had been a professor at the Riga Conservatory for nearly twenty years), and "a young cellist" performed the Tchaikovsky Piano Trio, the one Lev had played for Daliba Jones on his first evening in Florence. Subtitled "In Memory of a Great Artist," the trio was written to commemorate Tchaikovsky's friend, the pianist Nikolai Rubinstein. Now the ghetto musicians were dedicating it to the memory of the first Jews who died in Riga and the surrounding towns. Hundreds of people crowded into the dilapidated hall to listen to the familiar and beautiful music, linking them back to their previous lives. During the contemplative opening bars, an SD officer entered the hall with two German shepherds at his side. He went to the back of the large room and stood with the dogs, listening to the elegiac and often plaintive passages. He remained there for the entire concert and left silently when it was over. Something of a folk legend developed around the memory of the deeply emotional evening. Some people said that Lev Aronson performed in that trio, but Godes remembered the young cellist "perished later on."

PLOT OF AN OPERA

Representatives of the different workplaces would come to the spot where Jewish workers assembled at dawn. Each group had its own SD sharführer who took charge, marching them "in a military way, chin up and left foot forward," out of the ghetto, into the city in the morning, and back to the ghetto late at night. Each morning the columns of workers were formed at the entrance to the ghetto, where they would be selected for "employment... the rich next to the poor, the doctor next to the shoemaker, the lawyer next to the tailor. . . . The only thing that counted was survival. Titles no longer mattered; it was insignificant if someone had been a doctor, professor, lawyer, engineer." There was no distinction between the educated or illiterate, the famous or unknown; it was a strange reversal from the hierarchical structure of a conservatory or orchestra in the outside world. After selection, some would be loaded onto trucks that would take them to the outside work sites. They would stand, perhaps thirty or forty of them, shoulder to shoulder in the open and roofless wooden lorry no matter the weather. The others walked in columns, sometimes accompanied by a German on a bicycle.

The workers left the ghetto gate at dawn and returned at night. A beautiful Jewish woman used to walk in the columns at the side of one of the men from the ghetto. She was refined looking, slightly smiling though there was mournfulness beneath her smile. Lev noticed that it showed "in the flicker of her eyes, in the hesitance of her walk, the way she held her body—you could see it in the corners of her lips."

One day, at Daugavasiela, she approached him, saying, "I know we're strangers, but I'd like to get to know you, just to talk, nothing more."

After that they would meet at the ghetto gate in the mornings, and one day her group was combined with Lev's column, proceeding to the *werkstätten* at Gestapo headquarters. As they marched through the streets—she toward the front of the column and Lev in the rear—Lev was concentrating on his own thoughts, preoccupied, and at first didn't hear when the woman cried out. But when he saw a guard strike her with a stick, almost knocking her off her feet, he looked more attentively, "although still detached, feeling no particular pity or sorrow." To himself, he thought, "A nice person, a good human being." Then he began to feel outrage.

At first they were separated at work and she was assigned to one of the other German officials. But when Kelpsch needed a cleaning woman, Lev went to her employer and said with some authority, "This woman's assigned to Kelpsch." The German released her, and in that way they began to work together.

As Lev grew acquainted with the woman, he became more impressed with her character, "a crystalline, pure spirit." Gradually a half-romance grew between them, "love in a senseless situation that led nowhere." She would ask him for small favors, things that wouldn't be too difficult to do. Little by little they talked about their dreams and emotions; she had very definite ideas and a whole vocabulary for the many categories and concepts of love.

As her situation grew worse Lev tried to help from a distance. Eventually, her husband was sent to prison, and he disappeared. She confided in Lev that as long as she was alive their friendship would sustain her. When Lev found himself in difficulties at work she reassured him: "Don't worry, I have the strongest faith you won't be arrested." Several days after that she vanished.

Lev looked for her. In desperation he asked for her, but even after liberation, he never heard word of her again.

DOING BUSINESS

For a while Lev's group worked "in the Gestapo's back yard," under the watchful eye of Truhe. On the side, the Jews made "secret rendezvous," contacting friends or partners who had been entrusted with billfolds, watches, or bracelets, instructing them to sell their valuables in exchange for food that could be hidden in secret pockets or inside a hat or a shoe and smuggled back to the ghetto and their families. The Gestapo Jews developed a hiding place in the cellar of a house across from headquarters. Their Christian friends brought labeled bundles so the workers knew which was theirs. Karl Westen, concertmaster of the orchestra, the violinist with whom Lev had played Handel-Halvorsen Passacaglia, was exceptionally dedicated. He kept a velvet pouch "containing some ten pounds of family jewelry and heirlooms, gold chains, diamonds, bracelets," which he would sell to buy food for the Aronson family and his old teacher, Professor Metz. He even came to the ghetto with smuggled food.

Occasionally, there would be freight cars of food— chocolate or cocoa—standing on the tracks "without a destination and without a locomotive." When the Jews discovered "such coffers from heaven," they'd empty them and "do business," organizing, trading, hiding, sharing, storing the precious commodities. The entire economy of the city of Riga was turned upside down, and all the materials of ordinary life—perhaps even the Amati—were now free-floating like objects in a picture by Chagall.

Chapter 7

Leading to Rumbula

DEATH OF CHIUTAN

Lev developed a reputation as a hard worker. He "would polish leather belts to shine like glass. Why take a chance?" One day he and a few others were called into the office of SD Officer Truhe. They were told that a number of specialists, "Jewish shoemakers, tailors, shirt-makers, painters, upholsters, and paper hangers, highly qualified in their professions, men and women," would be joining their group. They were going to be released from Zentralka since their skills could be used for a new "enterprise." The Gestapo Jews were going to convert a building, Ausekla iela, Number 3, into a factory that would supply goods for the Germans.

The large and elegant building, constructed in the time of czars, had once served as living quarters for Russian soldiers. After Latvian independence, the front portion, facing parkland, was used by the American embassy and was renamed Washington Platz. The apartments were grand—ten rooms, some of them—and many enjoyed a view of the Daugava River. In 1940 the building had been taken over by the Soviets, but before that it had been owned by a Jewish family named Misroch. Even up until June 1941 many of the apartments had been occupied by wealthy Jewish families. After the German occupation those tenants had only been allowed to remove necessities, perhaps a bundle of clothing; everything else was left in place. Now it would be called *Werkstätten der Sicherheitspolizei*, Workshop for the German Security Police.

Truhe chose Heinrich Schoenberger as *Judenältester* to represent the Jews and Lev was his assistant. Both were fluent in German. Schoenberger was a small man with sharp blue eyes. He came from a professional background; he'd been an accountant. He didn't talk very much. But when he spoke he pronounced his words quietly with a correct German accent. Among a few of the Gestapo Jews, there was resentment against Lev. Some of them distrusted his demeanor, "always walking proudly and well dressed in the streets," always with an air of self-confidence or arrogance. Others complained about his soft hands; after all, he'd been a cellist and not a craftsman, and they thought he didn't belong among the select group of the Gestapo werkstätten. But from their very first assignment cleaning the large apartments, Lev was determined to work with the others.

The Riga Jews assigned to the project scrubbed floors, washed windows, polished knobs "like professional house cleaners," and while they labored, their guards played cards. Now in close quarters, they noticed for the first time that three of their members didn't work on the Sabbath—they wore yarmulkes and whispered the prayers, even havdalah. It was all right; the Gestapo Jews were satisfied to find work in a house that provided cover for their black market business.

Occasionally, one or the other would go to the street, looking for friends who were bringing packages. When Chiutan was spotted pacing back and forth on the pavement, Lev left the window he was washing and ran down the stairs to greet him. The Chinese wrestler looked careworn and thinner; his eyes were sad. Then he opened his jacket and food was inside. Lev embraced him and took the tightly packed bundles. For a few minutes they exchanged news. Chiutan was resolved to come to the entrance of the ghetto every morning and follow Lev to his destination. He would deliver messages and notify others about where the Gestapo Jews could be found so as many as possible would receive packages. In this way he would provide a link between the ghetto and the outside world.

That evening, when they completed the work of cleaning Ausekla, the men were separated from the women and taken in trucks to a loading spot for machinery, "all types of sewing machines, chairs, sofas, lumber, nails, hammers, saws, textiles, and furs," which would become the foundation for the production workshops. They packed up the trucks, making the trip back and forth to Ausekla four times. At the end of the day, the trucks brought the exhausted Jews back to the ghetto gate, which was guarded by Latvians. The Germans pushed their workers through with their packages smuggled under their clothes, saying, "These are our Jews and don't give them any trouble."

But the next day was different. After work only one German accompanied them to the ghetto gate. When he left, the Latvian guards saw their opportunity. They searched each of the Jews, confiscating hidden food as well as anything left over from their rations. Then they beat them viciously with clubs and sticks, "cursing at the top of their lungs,"

In the morning, the Jews complained to Truhe, who only shrugged it off. Reluctantly, they sent messages to their Christian contacts. It was useless to receive packages since the ghetto guards would take everything at the gate. That evening, at the entrance to the ghetto, the Latvian guards began beating the Jews again. When they realized there was nothing to steal, "they started a massacre," punching, whipping, and kicking. But suddenly they heard the shot of a pistol and everyone fell silent. Chiutan lay on the pavement in a pool of his blood. The guards had killed him because he had tried to stop the slaughter.

RETURNING TO THE GHETTO GATE

Again, as acknowledgment to his past profession as a well-known performer—or perhaps because he wasn't trained in a craft—Lev was assigned the job of greeting customers, taking orders, and making sure they were filled.

One of the first customers, a high-ranking German officer, came into the shop for a fitting. He was interested in "the unusual enterprise" and amused by the bruises, cuts, and swollen eyes of the Jewish clerks.

"What happened? Did your wives beat you?"

When he heard about the Latvian guards he made a flourish with his hand: "Those swine! Something should be done about them!"

Later in the day a German policeman came in: "Tired, dusty boots, rather short, fish eyes, bushy brows, dark hair, little on the plump side." He asked many questions that were the giveaway that he'd come from another city "and was looking for something."

"What's this operation?" he asked Lev. "And your background? A cellist? And the others?" His seeming naïveté "broke the ice" and Lev began to explain the situation with the Latvian guards. The German policeman listened carefully and then suggested, "Let me come with you this evening so I can see what happens."

As he had promised, at the end of the day he returned to accompany them back to the ghetto. At the gate, the Jews began emptying their coat pockets for the customary searches. But the German police officer pulled over the Latvian guards: "You won't lay a finger on these men! If I hear complaints, I personally will shoot you down like rats!" They saluted him as though he were their commander, and the Jews from Ausekla passed through the entrance unharmed.

SCHERWITZ

The German policeman called himself Fritz Scherwitz. Although he had been on his way to the Eastern Front, he abruptly changed his plan. In Riga he joined the SD and eventually took charge of the operation at Ausekla, moving into renovated rooms on the second floor, dressing in finery produced in the workshop, and expanding the enterprise to employ close to a hundred Jewish workers (eventually many more). Under his stewardship Ausekla became "a sample of German ingenuity, a center of unique achievement."

Scherwitz organized the operation for his own benefit, but he was unusually solicitous of the Jews who labored for him. For example, he warned his workers before there were inspections in the ghetto so they could hide food and smuggled goods in advance. He knew many languages and sometimes Hebrew and Yiddish words slipped into his conversation. He knew the words to Jewish songs, occasionally singing along with his workers. Lev noticed how he shrugged his shoulders and gestured with his hands like a Jew. He didn't talk about his past but took an interest in other people's stories.

On different occasions Scherwitz asked Lev about his background, family, and education, as though there was something in the details that jogged his memory. In November he allowed Lev's sister to join the werkstätten. Scherwitz especially wanted to hear Lev's stories about Berlin, with its movie palaces, concerts, and cabarets. After each question, Lev's memory of the past clarified, and things he thought he'd forgotten came to the surface. He described the mood of the city as he arrived off the train, "green and without experience," the cello under his arm. He talked about the musicians he had known from the conservatory and in jazz and theater, Brecht and Piscator, the "after concert" conversations that would go on all night, his friends from Peters, lessons with Piatigorsky. Once again he was reconnected to music, to a thread of the past, and even to the Amati.

29 NOVEMBER 1941
RIGA

The Riga ghetto had been sealed on October 25. By the middle of November there was no longer bread or meat in ghetto stores, only withered carrots, parsnips, and cabbage. Everyone was hungry and winter had come early. People were burning furniture for firewood and cutting down the few trees in the ghetto. Even though it was forbidden—when living quarters were searched people were shot "on the spot" for smuggling—the Ausekla Jews brought wood and logs inside the gates. At night there were many robberies. Anything valuable—silver, money, and jewelry—was wrapped in linen sacks, stuffed in tin cans, waxed closed, and buried in the ground. Every day as the workers assembled at the gates, they noticed more guards and officers stationed in the ghetto. Small groups were arrested, taken to Zentralka, and held as ransom, perhaps to forestall ghetto resistance. Random workers were taken into the Bikernieki pine forest and never returned. A group of women was "dragged to the beach and killed." When the Jews at Ausekla asked Scherwitz what was going on he made up lies: "They must have disobeyed regulations."

On November 29 Scherwitz assembled his people. He announced they wouldn't be going back to the ghetto that night. Instead they would sleep at Ausekla. There would be blankets, pillows, and food in the workshops. "Don't worry about your families," he said. "I was in the ghetto this morning, and I'm going back to see that they're managing."

For several nights, the Jewish workers remained at the werkstätten, but nobody could concentrate. Separated from their families, everyone became lethargic; there was "a general mourning" and a disjointed remembering of the past. Lev could recall the day the guards had come for his cellos. Before the knock at the door, he'd been practicing. His father had been in the room, and Lev was playing scales. Even scales can be beautiful, he liked to say, if you think of them as traveling up and down. He remembered his father listening to the Amati. Then, dispirited, Lev thought about his father, weak, lying in bed in the ghetto apartment. That's where the old man had been the last time Lev saw him. Lev and his sister were on their way to work and didn't want to disturb his sleep. Lev had bent over his father and taken a cigarette from his case. He was sorry about that now. His mother, leaning against the wall, wept.

Days passed, but the Ausekla Jews didn't go back to the ghetto. Scherwitz continued to reassure them about their relatives, but no one believed him. At night they slept in the top story of the house, where "everything was in a very primitive way; just to sleep; occasionally wash, shave, and work." They received small portions of kasha, hot cereal, rice, and bread from the kitchen.

Lev Aronson and his sister Gerda, c. 1916

Portrait of the Aronson Family, Riga, 1920

(Grün Studio)

Lev Aronson and Gregory Fomin, Jurmala, c. 1929

Lev Aronson with young musicians, Germany, c. 1929

Lev Aronson with the conductor Lovro von Matačić,
Jurmala, August 1932

Lev Aronson with Genya, Paris, January 1934

MELNGALVJU ZĀLĒ

Trešdien, 1937. g.

27. janvārī
plkst. 20

I. Sonate G-mollā . . . . Henri Ekkles
>   Largo
>   Allegro spirito (courante)
>   Adagio
>   Vivace

II. Koncerts D-dūrā . . . . Jos. Haidns
>   Allegro moderato
>   Adagio
>   Allegro Rondo

III. Sonate Op. 65 . . . . Fr. Šopēns
>   Allegro moderato
>   Skerco (Allegro con brio)
>   Largo
>   Finale Allegro

IV. a. Noktirne . . . . Šopēns-Piatigorskis
>   b. Habanera . . . . Ravels
>   c. Baal–Šem (Nigun) . . . . Blochs
>   d. Rekuebros . . . . Kassado

Pie klavierēm: Prof. P. Šūberts

Bechšteina koncertflīģelis no
Neldnera mūzikāla veikala

Sp. „Perfekt" Rigā, Jāņa ielā 5

OPPOSITE:
Program for Concert at Melngalvju nams, 27 January 1937

ABOVE:
Lev Aronson, Concert at Melngalvju nams

Lev Aronson with friends (violinist Karl Westen on the right), Riga, c. 1938

(V. Sules)

Lev Aronson with Joseph Schmidt aboard ship to Oslo, c. 1937

(H. Neibergs, Riga)

ABOVE:
*Lev Aronson with musicians (violinist Ruven Stender, center left,
and conductor Janis Kalninsh on the right), Libau, 1939*

OPPOSITE TOP:
Identification document, Berlin, issued 8 July 1946

OPPOSITE BOTTOM:
Diploma from Klindworth-Scherwanka, reissued November 1946

Personalausweis

Personalausweis Nr. _Ar/673/46_

Name: _Arnoff - Aranson_
Vorname: _Leo_
Beruf: _Cellist_
geboren am _7. Februar 1912_
in _München - Gladbach_
Staatsangehörigkeit: _Deutschland_
Wohnung: Berlin - _Zehlendorf,_
Potsdamer Chaussee 19

Abdruck
rechter Zeigefinger

Gebühr: _2.— RM_

Gestalt: _groß_
Gesicht: _oval_
Augenfarbe: _blau_
Haarfarbe: _dkl. blond_
Besondere Kennzeichen: _kein_

Unterschrift des Inhabers

Leo Arnoff-Aranson

Mit Ablauf des _7.2. Juli 1947_
wird dieser Ausweis ungültig, falls er nicht verlängert wird.

Berlin, den _8. Juli_ 1946

Der Polizeipräsident in Berlin
Polizeirevier _161_
Im Auftrage
Reinke

Eintragung der Kinder unter 15 Jahren umseitig.

Konservatorium der Musik Klindworth-Scharwenka

Konservatorium der Musik Klindworth-Scharwenka   Den 16.12.46.

Direktor: Walter Scharwenka
Stellvertr. Dir.: Georg Winkler
Hauptinstitut: Berlin-Charlottenburg
                   Berliner Straße 39
Zweiginstitut: Berlin-Friedenau
                   Kaiserallee 84
Fernsprecher: 32 45 26

Bescheinigung

Herr — Frau — Fräulein Lew Arnoff- Aranson

geb. am 7.2.12. in München - Gladbach

wohnhaft Zehlendorf, Potsdamerchaussee 19

studiert an unserem Konservatorium Musik. seit dem 23.11.45

Hauptfach: Cello., Dirigentenkl. Nebenfächer: Orcheste

XXDiese Bescheinigung gilt zur Vorlage bei XX

Nina Bukowska dancing, Liebestraum, 1946

Lev Aronson with Karl Westen, Hamburg, 1946

Gregor Shelkan and Lev Aronson, cover photograph for
"Der Durchgemater ter Weg," published in Berlin, c. 1946

Nina Bukowska, Rachel at the Well, *Berlin, 1947*

Lev Aronson, Berlin, 1947

(Gaza Studio, Berlin, and William Langley, Dallas)

Lev Aronson and Gregor Piatigorsky, New York, 13 April 1948

(*Herald Tribune*—Kavallines)

Chapter 8

After Rumbula

ADJUSTING TO TRAGEDY

Through some Latvians, the Jews at Ausekla heard rumors, "but they couldn't believe them." One day an inebriated German officer came to pick up his coat, and when he was told it wasn't ready he began cursing: "Useless filth! You should have been working like we were, overtime, dragging thousands of corpses. You should have been murdered with them. We'd have fewer mouths to feed. If my coat isn't ready tomorrow, this building will be swimming in blood like the ghetto!" His voice was so loud, everyone in the building heard. Then he slammed the door.

There was pandemonium. People were howling. Some lay on the floor. A few tried to commit suicide. When Scherwitz arrived and heard what the German had said, he stood in front of the Ausekla Jews, stunned at the way they had been told about the atrocities. Some thought he was angrier about the words of the drunken officer than about the killing.

During the next days, they sent messengers back and forth through the network of Jewish werkstätte in Riga and heard more rumors about the killing pits in Rumbula

Forest, the carnage in the ghetto, and the transports coming to Riga with Jews from the Reich countries. At night they slept together on the cold floor covered with only a thin quilt. Scherwitz was worried but tried not to display his concern. One day he came with a "carload of food—bread, cheese, butter, ham, salami, several cases of wine, a bottle of vodka, and beer." After locking the door, he announced they should stop working. He instructed the women to prepare supper from the food.

Slowly, the Jews in the werkstätten began to adjust to the tragedy. Lev took occasional solace from some brave Christian friends. The publisher Helmar Rudzitis lived across from Ausekla. He invited Lev into his apartment to use the telephone and send messages to the few surviving Latvian Jews scattered in the city. Once he arranged for colleagues from the opera—conductors, dancers, and musicians, including Mariss Vetra and his Jewish wife, whom he was hiding—to come by "for moral support." There were legends—some of them far-fetched—circulating about music at Rumbula. The death of the beautiful violin prodigy Sarah Rashina touched many people. She had been married to Gregor Shelkan, the tenor who sang in the National Opera. In 1937, the same year David Oistrakh took first prize, Rashina had been awarded a diploma at the Ysaÿe Competition in Belgium. It was said the old queen was so impressed by her performance that she filled the lovely young woman's pocketbook with crown francs. Now they said she had died in a conflagration; others whispered that she played her violin in the killing pit. There was a report that one of the Arajs men, like the pied piper, had played Chopin's funeral march on a mandolin while leading the last Jews to a spot in the old cemetery where they were shot.

AUSEKLA UNDER RUDOW

Lev was no longer part of the Jewish leadership. Boris Rudow became head of the werkstätten. Rudow was an elegant and flamboyant operator and a man with several past lives. Like Lev, he had come from a Jewish family in Latvia and traveled to Berlin in the 1920s. There he had danced at the El Dorado bar, made his way as a gigolo, and advanced in society as "a bogus baron." Like Lev, he had returned to Riga for military service and had many friends in the arts. He settled down and studied fashion design, working for a firm that sent him to London, Paris, and Rome to purchase fine fabric. Later, as an accomplished tailor, he became wealthy enough to establish his own shop. Rudow had been arrested at the beginning of the German occupation but earned his release because his expertise was needed at Ausekla. Once he joined the operation, the business developed into an establishment that provided "complete clothing for men and women," and all the Gestapo men became clients. Rudow knew where to find the confiscated tools and sewing machinery that had once belonged to Jewish factory owners and businessmen, and he knew the most accomplished tailors and seamstresses, requisitioning them from Zentralka, saving their lives. For his part, Scherwitz allowed Rudow to go without the yellow star, "for the dignity of the enterprise." Rudow fabricated a story that he been a Christian orphan raised by a Jewish family.

Riga was brimming with confiscated goods. Approximately 20,000 Jews, mostly women and children, from Germany and Czechoslovakia were arriving on deportation transports, and the property they carried on their backs and in suitcases was added to what had been stolen from Latvian Jews. Richard Dannler described the storage in his Nuremberg testimony: "In a large warehouse in Riga, I saw huge piles of clothes, some of it drenched with blood. I estimate this was part of the personal effects of at least 30,000 people." The better items ended up in Scherwitz's enterprise, where they would be cleaned and mended. Now Ausekla operated like a department store and a factory, providing goods for upper-echelon Germans. The ground floor showcased fine clothing, taffeta gowns, evening dress, and furs. An entire room was set aside as storage, and every item was labeled on index cards. Suitcases, collected when the trains unloaded in Riga, were arranged in the back rooms, stickers still bearing addresses from Hamburg, Vienna, Cologne, or Kassel.

Rudow received his SS and SD customers on the second floor, where there was a kitchen and pantry, dressing rooms, and living quarters. He and his family were granted the extraordinary privilege of living on the premises rather than inside the ghetto. Scherwitz and his Jewish mistress kept another apartment in the building, this one with high ceilings and a balcony.

Specialized Ausekla workshops producing uniforms, tuxedos, hats, underwear, gloves, shoes, and boots were housed on the third and fourth floors. At first these goods were produced from materials stolen from closed-down Jewish businesses. But as the operation enlarged and became embedded in the larger black market, their sources included all of Latvia. Scherwitz and Rudow even developed a private "side business," selling leather and soles for leather boots to Latvian black marketers, lining their pockets by selling to those they had stolen from.

In the attic there were six small bedrooms where the workers lived "until the ghetto became less crowded." Scherwitz allowed his workers to wear some of the stolen clothes, and he also made the goods available so they could trade on the black market. The Jews would smuggle desirable garments out of Ausekla, layering them under their tattered work clothes. Even warm underwear and socks could be traded for food with Latvian civilians.

Occasionally the Jewish musicians gave performances in the reception area that had a piano. Lev and his student Gus Geoffey were among the entertainers, playing before an audience of the dispossessed, surrounded by goods stolen from the dead. "We had to accept our fate," he said later, "and make the best of it."

WINTER 1941–42

RIGA

By all accounts the winter of 1941 to 1942 was extraordinarily harsh. About 5,000 remaining Latvian Jews were spread throughout the city in werkstätte or slave labor camps in the countryside. About half of them lived in the *kleine ghetto*, the little ghetto that was separated by barbed wire from the larger ghetto that held the Jews transported from the Reich countries. Jewish men and women were put to work removing snow from Riga's streets. They wrapped rags around their shoes and hobbled through the drifts. Lev noted, "Not one Latvian extended the smallest help to these workers." Like everyone else, Lev was witness to a thousand acts of cruelty. One day, Manana, a sailor working in the kitchen of the werkstätten, stole food for some Jewish women. When the Germans came for him, the young man lunged at them with a butcher knife, shouting: "For my mother, for my father, for all of us!"

Lev had no interest in music, which had once been his whole life. But in the warmer months musical instruments, like everything contraband, began circulating around him. Abram Schapiro—"Pimpelchen," or little dwarf—had a small mandolin he had stuffed in his pocket when he first entered the ghetto. Rudow and the pianist Leo Schalit had guitars. The Springfield brothers had a violin and a balalaika. They joined with a school friend and some of the Reich Jews to perform popular music and American-style jazz. Among the Reich Jews, there were enough musicians to form a small orchestra. Erich Eichenbaum, a violinist who had been a member of the Vienna Philharmonic, incredibly carried his own fine-quality Italian violin into the German ghetto, and Percy Brand, from Libau and Riga, also had a violin. SS Obersturmführer Kurt Krause supplied a cello that had been "abandoned" with the luggage belonging to someone from Dortmund who was killed at Salaspils. Later Krause requisitioned more instruments from the storehouses. Sunday afternoon concerts were held in the German ghetto. Professor Metz, whose wife had died in Rumbula, performed as a soloist.

AUTUMN 1942
RIGA

Maybe it is what I went through in the war that makes this piece so vivid for me, so close to my heart. When I play it, I play it in memory of all the people who gave their lives for nothing. . . .

To really respond to an experience like Schelomo, *perhaps it takes knowing that the Torah is not just a sacred scroll of parchment. You have a special feeling for it when you have helped to smuggle it into a ghetto under the nose of the Nazis so that you can celebrate the High Holy Days. When it is a matter of life and death, and something you are willing to risk your life for. . . .*

Schelomo: Rhapsodie Hebraique, with the deep and meditative voice of Solomon breaking through the dissonant rumblings of Ecclesiastes, always took Lev back to the fall of 1942. That autumn, some of the young men from the Latvian kleine ghetto considered various forms of resistance. Lev's friend from the opera, Gregor Shelkan, was one of them. After Rumbula, when Shelkan's wife and her relatives had been murdered, he and twelve other

Jews were living in the cellar of their workplace outside the ghetto. Two things played on their minds continuously: obtaining food and weapons, and "not to die as sheep." A resistance group was being organized among members of Riga Ghetto's Jewish police. Workers on the inside constructed bunkers beneath sheds, outbuildings, and within the walls of ghetto houses. Those who worked outside the ghetto stole hand grenades, dismantled rifles and pistols, ammunition, and "old vintage" machine guns. Much of their booty was taken from Pulvertornis, the fourteenth-century Powder Tower in the old city. They found a small canon in a supply depot, took it apart, and smuggled it into the ghetto in pushcarts and crates. Shelkan had always been interested in machinery. When he was a choirboy in Libau, he had an uncle, a watchmaker, who taught him how to do repairs. In Vienna, he had supported his studies at the conservatory with his skill as a watchmaker. Now he stole a large automatic weapon and rounds of ammunition. Patiently he disassembled it, storing it, piece by piece, in small boxes, giving each to a different friend to smuggle back to the ghetto. But the plan failed. On October 29, forty-one members of the Latvian Jewish police were killed, shot execution-style, on Tin Place in the German ghetto.

KAISERWALD

In March 1943, twenty months after the occupation of Riga, the Germans began the construction of K.Z. Kaiserwald in Mezaparks, a northern suburb of Riga. It was their intention that survivors of the two Riga ghettos, as well as those in the outlying werkstätte and slave labor camps—eventually, also, Jews from Vilna, Libau, Daugavpils, Kovno, as well as some from Hungary—would be transferred there. Kaiserwald was a concentration camp and completely different from the ghetto. The camp was under the command of Germans who had come from Sachsenhausen. When the Jews entered the gates, professional criminals, prostitutes, and pimps were in charge. As *kapos*, they were superior to the Jews, beating them with sticks, kicking them, and screaming obscenities. The few belongings that had survived the ghetto were taken away before the prisoners were sent to showers and their clothes were exchanged for rags. Instead of the "zebra clothing," which the kapos wore and which the Jews would get later when they were deported to other camps, a large X was painted across the front and back of their jackets and a white stripe was painted along their pants. Women's hair was cut short, and men's hair was shaved close. Families were divided, men separated from women. Everyone was assigned a number.

The most brutal kapo was simply referred to as Mister X, though later he was identified as Xavier Abel. There were many accounts of his past misdeeds—Lev believed he had been "apprehended in the greatest bank robbery in German history." At Kaiserwald he wore "an exquisitely tailored uniform of prisoner's cloth . . . high boots, in the officer style, and a blue beret." He supervised construction of the camp latrines as well as a sports hall for his own use. After the gymnasium was built, he sometimes called ten or fifteen young Jewish men to stand with their faces to the walls of the large, empty room so he could use their heads as punching bags.

Before long, most of the prisoners became sick with dysentery, and soon there was an epidemic of typhus. Naked corpses lay on the ground or were delivered to a pigsty before being carted to mass graves.

Lev entered Kaiserwald in the early summer of 1943. One night there was a strange performance. When the prisoners were asleep in the men's barracks, several Gestapo men, returning from an evening "with much drinking and revelry," decided to have some fun. They drove their cars inside the camp, parking in a semicircle facing the barracks. With a signal, headlights were turned on and guards screamed: "Everyone must evacuate the barracks!" Dazed by the light and partly asleep, the prisoners sprang to the door, but the door had been locked. As the commands continued, they crowded to the windows and pushed their way out where they were met by kapos who beat them with rubber truncheons. They were told to stand in line, and they were beaten. They were ordered: "Back to the barracks!" They crawled through the windows and were beaten again. This was a "carnival." It was repeated again every ten minutes for over an hour while spectators, men and women, looked on, laughing. Witnesses described one other performance at Kaiserwald. Gregor Shelkan was rewarded an extra bowl of soup after singing some songs.

LENTA

Luckily Lev remained at Kaiserwald for only a short time before he was transferred as a slave laborer to *SD Werkstätte Lenta* on the other side of the river. Lenta, a large factory and quartermaster supply depot, was an extension of the Ausekla workshops and still managed by Scherwitz and Rudow. Now it employed more than nine hundred Jewish workers. Furniture production and automobile repair had been added to the enterprise. Like the HKP factory in Vilna and Schindler's factory in Cracow, Lenta was a relatively humane workplace, considered the best assignment for the dwindling Jews in the Riga-Kaiserwald system. Supposedly only specialists were assigned to Lenta, and consequently Lev presented himself as a tailor, shoemaker, and "stocking knitter." He learned that wool was handled in skeins that needed to be rebundled on the spindles. He became a machinist for the spindle-winding machine. Operating with tools that had once belonged at Benya Hahn's knitting factory, he made socks and underwear.

Lenta consisted of a sprawling factory building of block architecture with barbed wire installed above the brick façade. There were several outbuildings and garages but in the main building, there was an entire floor of dormitories. Although men and women worked together in the factory, as in the main camp of Kaiserwald, they were separated in barracks at night. After all they had experienced, it was impossible not to feel that death was hanging over their heads; everyone knew they might be killed at any time, and many lived with the desire to fill the remaining time with as much experience as possible.

There was a piano on the second floor of the factory and, to raise spirits of the workers, Lev, Leo Shalit, and Mendel Basch sometimes performed. Scherwitz invited Shelkan to join them, and he sang several times for the Lenta Jews and the Germans. Sometimes Abram Schapiro played his mandolin. One concert, attended by many SS dignitaries, stood out among the others in the common memory. Basch accompanied his father, who sang arias from Verdi's *Don Carlos* and Yiddish songs. Shelkan sang the famous "Give Me Freedom," from Borodin's *Prince Igor*, in Russian. And some remember Herman Godes, Professor Metz, and Lev playing the beloved Tchaikovsky Piano Trio, the audience listening as they had in the first days of the Riga Ghetto, as though they were hearing a requiem for all who had perished. But Lev remembered differently. He said he never touched a cello during the war. In the autumn Professor Metz died at Kaiserwald.

Many romances occurred among the slave laborers, and the old standards of bourgeois morality fell by the wayside. Everyone wanted the comfort of someone to love, even if just for the moment. Middle-aged women applied the equivalents of rouge and lipstick to make themselves pretty, hoping for companionship. On one occassion, a young woman from Hanover came into the room where Lev was operating the spindle-winding machine. She came "with a mop and bucket to wash down the floors"; she was dressed in tattered clothes. Lev noticed her lovely face; dark, almost raven-colored hair; blue eyes; and long, tapering fingers. She must have been twenty years old. He began to talk to her, and she answered shyly. It didn't take long for Lev to offer her part of his rations and, "as a gentleman," he helped her mop the floor. Later, with Rudow's assistance, Lev arranged for her to become one of the machine operators so they could be together during breaks from work. When he was with her, Lev studied her hands, "beautifully lined" and "symmetric." They reminded him of the wax hands he had seen in Paris, resting on the ledge while the wind blew against the curtains above them. He watched the beautiful way she used them when she smoked, the cigarette butt balanced between the third and fourth fingers of her left hand. It was so elegant that Lev would "touch her hands to be sure they were real." In time she became friends with Lev's sister and with Gerda's fiancé. After work, they'd meet together; walking in the factory yard, talking. Eventually, with several other couples, they formed a group. Sometimes, to keep spirits up, they'd plan an imagined future, a steamship they'd take to America when the war was over. Once, imagining together the salt air on the ship deck, they began, slowly and rhythmically, to lean back and forth, side to side, with the motion of waves.

The girl with the beautiful hands scavenged fabric scraps, hundreds of tiny pieces, off the floor and sewed them into a scarf as a gift for Lev. Then she constructed a similar pair of gloves. At first, Lev was afraid of being laughed at, and he wouldn't put them on. But she insisted he protect his hands from the cold so he could play the cello again "when you get out." With Rudow's help, Lev managed to thank her by procuring a skirt and sweater. Then, through his underground connections with his old friend the Latvian violinist Karl Westen, Lev obtained a comb for a gift. This was unheard of; no one else at Lenta had a comb. The young woman was elated. Up until now "her hair had hung in strands, combed as well as possible with her fingers." But one day, when it was announced that all the Jewish women would have their heads shaved, the gift lost its purpose. Though the women "took it bravely" and no one cried, Lev understood their humiliation, and he wanted to help them. Again, he turned to Karl Westen, who got "some better food" and several small scarves so the girls were cheered up and "began to resemble nurses, with little white caps on their heads."

The inmates at Lenta had more freedom and mobility than other Jewish slave laborers in Riga, and in several ways Lenta became a crossroads for information. Just like at Ausekla, the prisoners were engaged in "business." They stole goods from the factory and traded them through the barbed-wire fence surrounding the camp. In the Gestapo garages they developed an ingenious "watch system." At certain times of the day they would make sure the Germans "were under observation" and far from the shop where BBC radio was broadcast from the automobiles that had been brought for repair. One Jew would keep an eye on the Germans, "another stood fifty feet behind him, another, thirty feet from the second, and so on all the way into the garage" where someone would listen to the news and remember exactly what was said so it could be reported to the others later. If the Germans began to leave their quarters, the Jews would use the Hebrew word for six, *shesh*, as the codeword for danger. Through the BBC they learned of the German defeats in Italy and the Ukraine as well as the advancing Red Army. Some of the Lenta Jews even worked in Gestapo radio headquarters and were privy to secret communications between Riga and the homeland, and others were sent on errands in cars and trucks inside the city, where they would hear whatever rumors were circulating. In this way they learned of the evacuation of the Riga Ghetto in November 1943, when 3,000 Jews were transported to Poland and ultimately to Auschwitz. They also learned about the mass killings in July 1944 at Kaiserwald. They could reckon there were now only about 5,000 survivors from the two Riga ghettos.

DEPORTATION

The Lenta prisoners were awakened at midnight on September 25, 1944. It was the evening before Erev Yom Kippur. Dozens of trucks with soldiers arrived at the camp in pouring rain. Searchlights were turned on; everyone anticipated a massacre. Instead the prisoners were rounded up and crammed, shoulder to shoulder, into the trucks, which carried them across the river, into the city, and on to Riga Harbor, where they could see military cargo and industrial supplies being dismantled from open warehouses. The whole place was in chaos. During the preceding days, the Soviets had begun pressing in on the German army with 500,000 troops in the area of Latvia and Estonia, and there was pandemonium among German officials, with anguished troops pouring down from the north.

A steamship was docked at the quay, and in the darkness the pier was swarming with civilians as well as German soldiers, German war wounded, and prisoners from other camps. In their ragged clothes, the prisoners stumbled into the teeming rain and formed a line, snaking along the quay. "Load the cargo!" someone shouted, and they began the work of evacuating Riga Harbor.

When the prisoners completed the work, they were ordered on board the small ship and then "driven down" into the cargo hold, "packed like herring in a barrel." More than a thousand prisoners—men, women, and children—lay on the steel grating or on a little sand on cold, wet planks. Lev remembered later how he watched a patch of sky through a "small hatch overhead." He listened to the steady sound of Russian aircraft from above and the occasional sound of the defending German anti-aircraft. He felt the ship list, and he became nauseated from the "crowding and the rolling of the boat." In the distance he could hear the boom of Russian warplanes "and the small German anti-aircraft in defense." The sea was rough, and the ship had to trace its path between the minefields the Germans had set. In the turbulence everyone became sick, defecating and vomiting wherever they lay. The smells were ghastly. Many people died that day, and the corpses were thrown into the sea. At sundown, Lev's friend from the Riga Opera, Gregor Shelkan, began to sing the melody of Kol Nidre. In the hold of the steamship, Lev must have half-heard the voices of the cantors from his childhood in Voronezh and Riga and the magnificent voice of Joseph Schmidt, who had traveled with him to Oslo. The Bruch concerto was still in his fingers. He had certainly played it on the Amati. Some of the suffering passengers joined in chanting the atonement prayer, "tears flowing freely."

They remained in the cargo hold for several days, as the ship made its way through turbulent waters along the Baltic coast, past Memel and Konigsberg, dodging Russian fire. There was no water for blistered throats and lips until the guards turned high-pressure hoses on them as if they were livestock, and the hatches were uncovered so that pots for waste were delivered down.

When the German steamship finally docked in Danzig Harbor, hatches were opened and they disembarked. One of the German Jews whispered under her breath, "Now we're on our own soil," but the ordeal was only beginning. The prisoners were made to unload the freighter. Then, escorted by guards with whips, they were marched toward the Vistula. As they proceeded, they saw a truck filled with American POWs skidding past them, and they heard the men shouting in English: "Try to escape! Death in the forest will be better than where you're going!" At the river they were loaded on barges once used for carrying sand and rocks, now connected by chains. They glided where farmland stretched flat along the rim of the river, and workers in the fields stopped to watch the strange sight. The prisoners stood in the cold, dressed in the filthy remnants of jackets and trousers, some of them barefoot, women in torn skirts or dresses, a few wearing men's jackets or with scarves covering their heads. Abram Schapiro still had the "little broken down mandolin" and a guard told him to play "La Paloma":

> *. . . if I die and, over the ocean's foam,*
> *a white dove comes, gently, on a fair evening,*
> *open your lattice, dearest, for it will be me,*
> *my faithful soul . . .*

Some of the farmers must have touched their throats, making the slicing gesture of a knife. No one moved or returned to work until the barges were out of sight.

Chapter 9

Stutthof

Thirty-five kilometers to the east of Danzig, encircled by wetlands and channels, bogs and sloughs, the spit of land is almost completely inaccessible. The surrounding countryside is covered with mounds of sandy hills dotted with slanting birch and withered pine, ditches and slopes, and bushes with thorns, prickles, and berries. Balys Sruoga, the Lithuanian poet, named it the Forest of the Gods: "once the bottom of the sea . . . as if during a storm the waves unexpectedly froze. . . ." Again, it brought Lev back to the floating and lonely first note before the mysterious opening crescendo of *Schelomo*. He looked through the camp gates, past barbed-wire fences and the trenches. He saw the Ukrainian guards walking with long whips, metal pipes, and sticks, followed by wolf dogs. He thought, as many had before him: "Abandon all hope, ye who enter here."

The Jewish prisoners from Riga passed through the latticed death gate, a barrier of barbed wire and electrified cable, crossing over "the old-fashioned cobblestones" and "the large, grassy plaza." The smell of burning mixed with the smell of the sea. Before them were rows of low, tent-like buildings with peaked roofs—"a field full of huts," as Lev and Shelkan described it in the elegy they would write together three years later. They passed the camp commander's garden and his brick residence with a flagpole. Someone screamed, "*Mutzen ab!*" (Remove your hats!) Suddenly a guard was on "the inattentive prisoner" who neglected to take his off, lashing him with his whip until he sank in the sand.

IMPRISONED BUT STRANGELY FREE

A student who faithfully does everything that his teacher tells him to may become an excellent instrumentalist but will be a poor teacher—however, one who has struggled to discover what is important is able to tell someone else. I was a good student, but I had a lot of time to start thinking about things when I was in the camps. I was imprisoned yet strangely free, because thinking was the one thing that couldn't be taken from me. . . . They couldn't tell if I was thinking or not. . . .

At Stutthof, Lev Aronson, once the owner of a cello made by Nicolò Amati, became "strangely free." It didn't occur all at once. Rather, it happened slowly and in stages.

DAILY LIFE

In the morning they were awakened at 4:00 a.m. They stood in front of their barracks while someone poured "coffee" made out of chicory from a wooden trough into a mess bowl. The glazed bowl was sometimes shared between two prisoners. When a trumpet sounded four times, the rough brass sound floating through the fog, they moved under gaslights, standing in "formations, ten rows, ten men abreast," four hours on their feet, sometimes doing deep knee bends, wondering, "How long, Oh Lord, how long?" Men were called for work, hauling stumps from the forest, pulling heavy wooden wagons through the sand. Everyone knew if they returned "bloodied and beaten" they were lucky. The others were carried on makeshift stretchers, constructed from the boughs of fir trees. *Appell* was followed by another trumpet, the warm buzzing breaking the silence. At noon: "soup" of muddy liquid, muddy cabbage or kohlrabi root, dirty peel swimming at the top. Observant Jews joked it was neither meat nor dairy. Evening: slice of bread made from wood dust.

BREAD

Barracks elders stand by the window, cutting the bread, their job. A loaf should produce sixteen slices like a measure with sixteen notes . . . but seventeen, eighteen, nineteen—that means the portions will be thin and the bread-slicers will "trade the surplus" for black market margarine, canned goods, or tobacco.

POCKETS

They entered Stutthof on Sunday but didn't receive uniforms until the following Wednesday. During that time they wore their clothes from Riga. Once, during roll call, a search was ordered: "Hands in the air!" Several Riga survivors were musicians, and they stood together. Guards went through the formations, confronting individual prisoners, searching "head to foot." Lev was "calm"; he stood "deep in the formation," comforted he didn't have anything to hide. After a while, from the raised platform, the commander announced: "Nothing's been found yet! Let's quit!"

Lev made his way toward the barracks with the man who'd been standing beside him. Suddenly the hand of this "friend of many years" grazed against the pocket of Lev's jacket. Without thinking, Lev brushed him away. The man gazed off. Then Lev felt it again.

"What's going on?" Lev reached inside his pocket and came up with something small, round like a lozenge. He remembered in Lenta some of the prisoners had taken ten-ruble gold coins and covered them with cloth so they'd look like upholsterer's buttons.

"Hand it over!"

"What?"

"It's mine. I'm the one who placed it in your pocket."

Lev was furious; this man he had known for years had put his life in peril. Then Lev made a fist deep in his pocket and felt something else: a handful of flints had been there since Lenta. He'd forgotten them. Now in Stutthof, "it was like finding an oil well." During the next days he shared the profits with his old cello student Gus, "the only one who would remember the little boys"—Lev's first students who had died in the Riga Ghetto.

MARKETING FLINTS

> *. . . have to make something for oneself.*

That evening and the next and the next, Lev and Gus, teacher and student, marketed the flints. First they traded for an extra portion of bread. Then "it was like Wall Street." As news spread, the price kept going up, so the two cellists survived on the flints for several days, making more with each trade until, finally, a French prisoner who had received a Red Cross package offered a salami for a flint. Lev was beside himself because he had just traded his last flint for "a bowl of soup and two portions of bread." The enticement of salami was beyond anything he'd dreamed of. He ran to his previous client and offered half the salami if he could buy back the flint. For a moment the man considered the stakes. "The salami won." He took the flint out of his lighter, entrusting Lev to negotiate with the Frenchman. But then everything went wrong. The Frenchman had disappeared, apparently frightened by the penalty for visiting Jewish barracks— twenty-five lashes with a whip. Lev and his cello student returned to the previous customer but found themselves in trouble again, the man "demanding his salami."

LAUGHING

Lev learned that with a five-ruble bribe a woman could be "bought out of the camp," transferred from Stutthof to a sub-camp where she could work as a slave laborer and have a better chance of survival. Lev thought he might save his sister's life. Some prisoners had made the transaction with gold teeth, but Lev didn't have dental work, and his sister had false teeth but no gold. He and Gus turned to the man with the cloth-covered gold piece: "You put my life at risk for ten rubles, now give me five to save my sister's life."

The man laughed.

WILL IT FALL?

About three hundred naked men and boys of all sizes filled the lavatory. There were showerheads on the ceiling. Attendants handed out a few "slivers of green-yellow soap." The water was turned on and off. A few drops hovered on the showerheads. Lev stood transfixed by a random drop: "Will it fall or not? Finally it fell."

END OF THE MANDOLIN

Abram Schapiro had stuffed his mandolin and an envelope of old photographs in a pocket. Now his clothes from Riga lay in a heap on the ground. When he reached for them a guard struck at him with the butt of his gun. But when the guard saw that the boy wanted photographs, he threw them over. The mandolin remained in the mound of clothes.

RECEIVING A NUMBER

Outdoors, three barbers with dull razors, slapping the men with stinging disinfecting solution. Uniforms were distributed: shirts, pants, jackets, caps, wooden shoes, paper to wrap delicately around the feet like socks. "Naked in wintertime, putting on the garments," vertical stripes, painted with phosphorous "to prevent escape by night." Everyone wore a number "preceded by a colored triangle": green for criminals, red for political prisoners, purple for *Bibelforscher* (Jehova's Witnesses), yellow for Jews. Lev was number 95,573. The opera singer Gregor Shelkan was 96,510.

IN DELIRIUM

Every minute of twenty-four hours surprises occurred.

*Sometimes in life things become so tragic
that nothing else remains but to laugh.*

Prisoners would come and go—some from the Hungarian territories, Slovakia, and Poland; a number were transferred to Stutthof from Auschwitz. New inmates barely elicited response since no one had energy to spare for curiosity; "a new bunch of prisoners was merely a new group in trouble." Then, one day, a group arrived from Riga, familiar faces, one of them "a former dandy." Though the admittance procedure was well established— selection, confiscation of clothing, showers, haircuts, distribution of prison garments—for a while the Germans had run out of uniforms and several days passed without new supply. "What's to be done? Regulations require a change of clothing, but no clothing's available." Finally, the authorities arrived at a novel solution. Near the camp a train was idled, and it was filled with goods that had been looted from the Soviet Union, including costumes stolen from a Russian opera theater. After the showers, the costumes were dispensed to the new prisoners: "Boris Godunov, Napoleon, Lion-tamers, Victorian dandies. Full dress suits walk across to the barracks. Some were mixed, half full dress, half-Boris Godunov." The dandy from Riga was dressed as a Caucasian Cossack.

RED CROSS

French and Italian POWs received Red Cross parcels. In the Jewish block . . . no one can send to us. . . . There is no one to send to us. This is why we have no right to be alive. . . .

One day it was learned that representatives from the International Red Cross would make an official visit to Stutthof. There followed a frenzy of preparation. Filth must be cleaned from the barracks, "everything polished, inside and out." New mattresses were requisitioned, the old burlap stuffed with fresh straw. On the day of the inspection there was a delay before the noon meal. Bells were ringing, "but still no commission." When the sealed lunch pails finally were opened there was a miracle: "chicken soup swimming in fat with carrots and celery." The prisoners, "with mess plates hung on ropes around their waists," almost swooned with joy— "What a prize for their hard work!" Each man walked gingerly, head down, to avoid spilling the soup from his plate. Thus concentrating, they didn't notice the teams of Germans formed on either side of the Jews. In an instant they were shoving the prisoners "back and forth between them, spilling the soup from the mess plates to the ground." The prisoners dived to the floor, trying to salvage the precious pieces of chicken, but the guards trampled on their fingers, squashing them under the heels of their boots. Lev no longer had musicians' hands.

LEARNING THE HARD WAY

Camp is a world of its own, differing in every way from life outside. At appell, newcomers stand in the first row. We were newcomers once. We had learned the hard way, in the first row one is exposed to a lot of danger, one might be selected for labor. . . .

TIME

Lev and a few other prisoners, some of the Riga musicians, were trucked to a place where there were "hills of coal." A guard threw shovels at them and ordered them to fill the back of the truck. He said to load it in an hour or they'd be shot and buried in the coal.

How should they pace themselves? How could they gauge their time? No prisoner had a watch. There were no clocks in the camp; "the concept of time did not exist in the camps."

Suddenly Lev had an inspiration. He could "think-sing" concertos. The concertos by Haydn, Boccherini, and Saint-Saëns were about twenty minutes long. Three together would make an hour. He tried bringing the music back in his head and, to his surprise, he remembered "every orchestra entrance, every fingering and bow stroke. Memory was remarkable, it was remarkable to remember. The shovel became my cello. . . . If I needed more time, I could sing the Dvorak Concerto. . . ."

IN THE "OPERA"

Prisoners were only permitted to use the latrine at night, accompanied by a guard. One evening, following regulations, Lev asked a guard to accompany him to the "opera." The guard waited by the door. When he was finished, Lev noticed "a treasure" on the floor of the latrine. He bent down and grasped the stamped-out stub of a cigarette, two inches long. Now he had a dilemma: How to light it? When the guard came to see if he was finished in the john, Lev explained his problem.

"Have you got fire?"

"All right, but snap it up."

Lev lighted his treasure, but just as he started to inhale the guard came back. "Hurry up, here comes the chief." Lev closed his hand around the burning butt of the cigarette and the officer saw the smoke in the darkness. "What do you have there?" "Found in the opera." "Found? So? Okay!" He drew a glove from his pocket "and slowly, carefully, meticulously" stretched his hand inside the leather before slapping Lev across the face.

THROUGH IMAGINATION

"I was never alone.... I talked to my friends every moment...." Through imagination Lev carried friends, especially friends from music, inside himself. In that way, he brought them along and they helped him absorb the pain. He would think, "Just see what a situation *we're* in now...."

THE BOX

".. . have to make something for myself. . . . To survive in the camp is an art. . . . One has to walk briskly, to shave with a piece of glass, look useful. . . ." Lev found a wooden box among some trash. It seemed like it might be useful, and he began walking with it on his shoulders. When he encountered a kapo who asked what he was doing, he answered: "An officer told me to bring this box to the Russian block." "Okay, go on," he said. Miraculously, the box had given him a cover.

Lev brought the box to appell. Deep in the formations, in the last row, he placed the box by his feet. At dismissal he left with the box on his shoulder and walked through the camp, carrying it. Suddenly, with the wooden box, he had an identity and he felt like a person again. From that point on he always carried the box: "I loved my box . . . my box was everything."

HOW TO THINK ABOUT TIME AND PATIENCE

A young prisoner, a Russian boy, lost his mind. One evening he ran all over the yard, screaming, "Death to Hitler! Death to Himmler! Death to all of you for taking away my father!"

With little difficulty the guards restrained him. Then the trumpet's shimmering brass was blown four times through the darkness. Everyone was awakened for appell illumined by gaslights. The men stood in formation beneath the gallows, and the guards brought up the boy.

"*Achtung! Mutzen ab!*"

It didn't take long for him to die. Afterward, no one said a word. Thoughts were conveyed just with the expression of the eyes or with a shrug.

Time becomes almost a solid thing. A definition for Time: "How to pass through today's time avoiding difficulties that lead to death." A definition for Patience: "It cannot last forever. The longer we maintain ourselves without losing life, the greater our chances for survival."

LEV'S DREAM

Lev dreamed about an enormous gate, part of it high and made of wrought iron, part the Elephant Gate in the Tiergarten. Lev remembered the Russian refugees of the 1920s, sleeping in the beautiful park, their instrument cases tucked under the bench. In his dream, the gate opened and prisoners marched "to safety." Then they were marching through mud, on dirt roads, finally highways. There was a sign that read: 3 km. Lev told his friends it was an "omen"; the dream meant they'd be liberated in three months. Everyone began counting the days.

ON THE MARKET

German civilians as well as officers were situated around a table raised on a wooden platform where the gallows normally stood for night executions. Camp commander Max Pauli stood on the dais. Lev noted, "In his gray field uniform with black patch collar trimmed in silver and with his high boots, [he] resembles Erich von Stroheim."

The command was given: prisoners were to run two hundred meters, the length of the yard. After a pistol shot, the men in their "striped pajamas" began running in a panic. It was almost impossible for many of them to cross the field. So many had dysentery or boils on their feet. Some were half-limping. Several had no shoes. The air was filled with clomping, wheezing, and crying. In the confusion Lev and many others fell in mud. He couldn't get a foothold. Men were trampling "wildly" over him. Finally he raised himself and managed to get across. Those who didn't make it were "herded together" and taken away. The ones who had proven they were able to work were now "on the market" as slave laborers.

Methodically, officials at the table announced: "auto mechanics, locksmiths, watchmakers, radio specialists, machinists," and one by one, men who had trained at those professions came forward. Lev stood beside two friends, the opera singer Shelkan and his student Gus. Lev said, "I guarantee they're not going to call for cellists. Next profession's mine."

"Are you mad? How can you put your head in the fire?"

"How can it be any more in the fire than now?"

"Welders!" the call came.

"Why not come with me?" Lev said to his friends.

The tenor followed, but Gus stayed behind.

Lev made his way to the table. Some of the Germans were comfortably seated and the others were gathered behind. Several prisoners formed a circle around the table.

"Welder?"

"Electric? Acetylene?"

"Electric and acetylene!"

"How long have you worked at these?"

"Twenty years."

"All right!"

Lev was now part of a labor unit that would leave the camp.

GERDA

That night Lev had difficulty sleeping; he knew he must say good-bye to his sister. In the morning after appell he went to the gate near the women's camp and asked one of the women to find Gerda. After a few minutes his sister came to the fence. She was hardly recognizable. Through the barbed wire Lev could see she was wearing rags and her eyes were glazed. She looked as if she were in shock. Her hand was covering her mouth and she was crying while her mouth was trying to produce words. Suddenly a female guard appeared at the gate and began hitting Gerda with a stick, shouting and cursing her until the girl pulled away. Her hair and face were matted in blood. She struggled to say something, then turned and ran back to the barracks.

LEAVING STUTTHOF

The long, opening note of Schelomo, *sound hanging in emptiness.*

Each prisoner turned in his plate, spoon, and rag used as a towel. Uniforms were stripped off. Two hundred naked men went to the shower. Paper-thin soap, perhaps twenty shards. Everyone begging, screaming, shouting for a piece of soap. Drops of cold water. This time the showerheads produced cold water. Then the barbers, lotion that burned the scalp, and new uniforms, but the same ersatz cloth made from paper: jacket, trousers, shirt. They stood in formations once again before their march. Lev glanced toward the women's camp, "instinctively knowing" he'd never see his sister again.

They were herded to the river and loaded onto a ferryboat. From a distance, the trumpet call. It was part of a choral taken from a church in Poland. At the end the trumpet played four times. There was a fuzzy sound with the last breath. Lev remembered the trumpeter facing north, south, east, and west.

Chapter 10

Schichau Werke

ERBARME DICH, MEIN GOTT

The boat was moored after sunset in Danzig. The men were ushered into a building with an enormous mess hall. They were commanded to take chairs set around long dining hall tables. The prisoners who had grown accustomed to hunger suddenly experienced a different kind of appetite, spontaneous and "automatic," caused simply by being in the vicinity of the dining room, by the body's memory of food served at a table. The men sat silently without moving for four hours, only slowly coming to understand that their sitting would have nothing to do with eating. The train that would carry them to the next camp was four hours late. The trip that should take one hour took twelve. Lev thought of the great Bach aria, "*Erbarme dich, mein Gott,*" Have mercy, my God.

7 DECEMBER 1944

DANZIG-BURGGRABEN

The night sky was completely black as they gathered at the gate. Floodlights suddenly came on, lighting up the scene. The men knew from experience that machine guns might be turned on them. Lev was still with Shelkan. The gates were opened, and they slinked inside. No shooting. The ground was spongy with large puddles and ditches of water all around. Some of the men lost their wooden clogs in the sludge. Another formation. Plate, spoon, and rag "re-issued." They were given bread, then led to barracks and beds—"Decided improvement—three across instead of four." There was a stove but nothing to heat it. The camp had no water.

THERE'S WORK FOR THEM

All morning and afternoon the men organized the camp, cleaning and sweeping. At 5:00 p.m. they marched to the nearby railhead and climbed onto freight cars that carried them to Danzig. From there they walked in their paper-thin uniforms through the dark and bitter cold for an hour and a half toward the sea.

By the wharf Lev could make out an enormous gate and a mountain of coal beneath billows of red smoke and haze. It was like a scene from *Götterdämmerung*. This was the shipyard where German submarines were built, Schichau Werke.

The prisoners from Stutthof crossed under the tall gate of the wharf and divided into small groups of six or seven men. Lev's group was escorted by a German soldier who marched them to a civilian foreman, an elderly man.

"Follow me to my office," he said. And to the soldier, "Wait outside."

The prisoners stood in a queue within his office while the foreman paced around them. From time to time he stopped and looked into the face of one or the other of the men. In a sudden outburst he said, "You're not welders. Don't lie to me. Perhaps you can dupe 'the big shots.' I won't be played with!" Then he paused: "If I had been you, I'd have said I was a welder too."

He walked to his desk where his breakfast had been set out: bread, butter, salami. He divided everything into seven portions and handed them around.

"Eat quickly. This is the first and last time I'll do this. I won't put my family in danger."

The faces of the prisoners flushed. It was unheard of to experience the slightest compassion.

Then he screamed: "Filthy pigs!"

Faces fell again.

"Those are the expressions I expect when you leave this room." He opened the door and said to the guard: "Agreed. There's work for them."

TOSSI

The boats in the shipyard were built across framed scaffolding, sometimes six stories high. Planks were laid inside the scaffolding to create work surfaces so construction could be done on many levels at the same time. On that first morning, Lev was brought before a short man with a beret. His face was dark with Mediterranean features and Lev guessed he might be Jewish. In fact he was an Italian prisoner of war.

The short man, whose name was Tossi, began to talk, and Lev could understand every word because of his time in Florence.

"You're not a welder," Tossi said.

"Yes," Lev insisted. "For twenty years."

Tossi shrugged, "We're both prisoners of the Germans. We have to work together. Want to smoke?" He raised a tin box off the floor and opened it. Inside there was tobacco and rolling paper. "Follow me."

They climbed high across the ship's scaffolding until they reached a protected area. "Up here." Tossi gestured for Lev to sit beside the tin box, which he opened again. Immediately they came to an understanding: one would gather tobacco and the other roll the papers. They smoked in silence for a long time. After a while Tossi brought out a small welding kit and began to heat a bit of corroded steel. He placed a field kettle on top of the hot metal. Within a few minutes they were eating warm spaghetti, the first "substantial food" Lev could remember.

"You're not a welder, and you'll be in danger if they find out. You must learn right away—I can teach you. Keep your wrist flexible when you handle the torch up and down, back and forth, smoothly, relaxed."

The movement was simple. The technique was similar to bowing.

"What's your profession?"

"Cellist."

"*Ecco, bravo, sono violinista!*" Tossi pantomimed a violin.

From that time on, there was "much singing of scores *con espressione*," while rehearsing the wrist movement of acetylene welding. Electric welding would come next.

HE ASKED ME TO FIND YOU

Every evening the Jewish prisoners traveled from Burggraben to the Schichau Werke at 8:00 p.m. It was bone-chillingly cold on the open water in midwinter. After three weeks the schedule was reversed. Now they began the trip at 4:00 a.m., arriving at the shipyard to work by day. In either case, they only viewed the wharf in twilight, sundown or sunrise, smoke ascending from the yards, tinted by the glow of hundreds of welding torches.

In the day shift, all the faces were different, and Lev was downcast to have lost his friend. But after the first day a man approached him. "Are you Aronson? I know Tossi. He asked me to find you. Follow me."

He brought Lev across the yard to the commissary that was used by the Italian prisoners. This new acquaintance arranged a job for Lev. From that point on, when food trucks arrived, Lev would unload them, carrying the large, sealed food vats up to the second floor where the POWs were fed. Each time he delivered the vats, he received a bowl of food as payment.

UNIVERSITY

In the shipyard, workers often needed to climb into the upper reaches of the submarines as they were being constructed. To do this, they used "ladders," steel plates that were positioned at an incline with small bumps of steel welded to the surfaces as traction. For a while it was Lev's job to do the spot welding for the ladders. The work was done with a loose wrist. He wasn't provided with any eye shield.

One morning he noticed a civilian standing over him, watching. The man wore a black jacket and trousers, the clothes of a common laborer. After a few minutes the man bent towards him, "I've heard you're a musician."

"I've worked as a welder for twenty years. Really, I don't know about music." Lev continued the spot welding.

Though shorter than Lev, the man was strapping. He had a broad nose, thick lips, and almost black hair. "Look, I'm also a musician, a clarinetist. But your friends told me you've been to conservatory. I have questions—if you tutor me I'll help you here in the shipyard."

"I'm a welder."

"If you were trained as a welder, you wouldn't botch this work. Will you teach me or shall I turn you in? Listen, trust me. Go to the locker area, and you'll see I've left something for you."

Lev went to his cupboard where there was a slice of bread. He returned with it to where the German was standing.

"Do you believe me?"

"Yes, but I'm not a musician. I know something about music . . ."

"Put down the welding. I'll do it."

For many weeks Lev and the new acquaintance worked in the shell of a submarine. The man was part German, part Polish, perhaps twenty-five or thirty years old. He did all the welding while asking questions: "What is a cadence? What are harmonic tones? What is a mode?" Occasionally, to impress others, he would scream out: "Goddamn swine, why can't you do this better?"

Kneeling on the steel plates, Lev told him about the history of music, century by century. Every day there were more question: "How did music begin? How do you learn by heart? What is coloration? Why are dynamics different in different composers' work? Can you play a Baroque piece with the same spirit as a Romantic work? Can you rely on the tempo marks?" With a piece of chalk he kept in his pocket, the clarinet player took dictation, writing on the newly welded steel. If the work was correct, Lev would erase it with the bottom of his shoe. Sometimes the clarinetist would bring passages from orchestral scores he collected at home, Mozart's Symphony in E-flat Major or Liszt's Hungarian Rhapsodies. Lev would explain theory and composition. If he spoke too loudly his student would warn, "Be careful or they'll shut down the university." At the end of each day the clarinetist would go home and write in a notebook everything he remembered from their lessons.

LEVY

Lev developed a chest cold and a wheezing cough. The clarinet player brought him an old jacket that he could wear beneath his striped uniform. It was tattered but lined with fur and provided warmth. Every morning Lev would slip it on quickly so the guards wouldn't notice. This went on until the prisoners' schedule was changed and they returned to the night shift.

Then Lev's illness became worse, and he was too weak to go to the ship wharf. At Burggraben, Lev was moved from the barracks to the infirmary. Several other Jewish prisoners were also sick: the Singerfeldt brothers as well as a Dutch Jew named Levy who shared a bed with Lev. The clarinet player heard about Lev's condition and was alarmed. In Danzig, he obtained sulfa pills for all four of the ailing Jews and arranged to have Lev's friend Shelkan smuggle them, wrapped inside newspaper, back to the camp.

Once they received the medicine there was still the problem of how to swallow the enormous pills without water. The Singerfeldt brothers, who were somewhat stronger than the others, were designated to go out in the snow every morning. Behind the barrack, they urinated, melting the snow. Then they'd bring back water in their hands so the men could swallow the large, red sulfa tablets.

When Lev began to recover he would talk for hours to the Dutch Jew, Levy. One evening Levy was full of deep questions: "What is the sense of life? The meaning of it? What makes the planets and all of the universe rotate? Is there a reason to fight for everything? All this struggle? Schmeling, like every other champion prizefighter, will get knocked down, and then where can he go?" After that he was quiet. Lev figured Levy had fallen asleep. He wrapped his arm across Levy's shoulder and closed his eyes. In the morning Levy was dead.

Lev returned to the shipyard, but a few weeks later the clarinet player was called up to the *Arbeit Dienst*, the Reich's work service. Lev never saw him again.

VIOLINIST FROM RIGA

There were new regulations: prisoners would no longer receive food from the shipyard. Now at mealtime they were marched to the railway station in Danzig, where rations were waiting. These were carried on poles back to the yard. When meals were finished the empty cans were returned to the station. At the shipyard they filled cans with water to bring back to the camp. In this way the Jews made many trips to Danzig every day.

One day, on the street, Lev noticed an acquaintance from Riga, a well-known violinist who had once been a friend. The man was wearing "a heavy black coat with a fur collar." In an instant, the man turned around so he was "concealed." Lev didn't understand the gesture.

Lev asked the guard if he could run back to this man—there might be something his acquaintance would give him—some cigarettes to be shared with everyone.

The guard agreed, but when Lev returned and caught the man's eyes, the violinist stared blankly and disappeared.

Chapter 11

End of the War

JANUARY 1945
POMERANIA
They set out in the last week of January 1945. Since the Russian troops were bearing down, the Germans were sending prisoners, thousands of them from the camps and subcamps, and "their keepers" west and north through Pomerania. They moved in nine columns across frozen ground, sometimes through an ice blizzard with powerful wind—the lucky ones still had shoes. A few walked with blankets. Sometimes they encountered prisoners from other camps. An accordionist miraculously walked with his instrument strapped to his back. At night they slept in empty buildings—barns or churches—deserted camps, or on the ground. The march had "no direction, no destination," often winding in circles and doubling back to avoid the Russian army, which was pushing deeper toward Berlin and into Germany. In one place a road sign would indicate *Lauenburg 10 kms* but they'd cross a field and a sign would say: *Lauenburg 90 kms.* Many fell down, exhausted, starving, and cold. They lay on the ground and guards shot them. At the head of the line, an automobile carried German officials on the lookout

for a stopping point. After ten days of "almost endless wandering," they found a camp that no one had heard of before. It was situated between the rivers Leba and Okalica. It appeared to be vacant. To be sure it "wasn't a trap," they sent an expedition of thirty *Oberjuden* "to investigate." One of them took the opportunity to escape, but the others reported back with assurances: the camp was "safe."

GOTENTOV

The prisoners were about four hundred miles west of Danzig in a place called Gotentov. The buildings were set on a hill, the main house and kitchen at the summit and rows of barracks in tiers beneath. A ring of forest grew at the base. The surviving Jews were now mixed with Christian prisoners. They slept in primitive barracks with a dirt floor, a small stove, and "shelves" to lie down on. There was very little food, and everyone was beside themself with hunger. Sometimes they would dig up a "semi-ripe" potato from a storage pit. Once or twice some of the prisoners came across a dead horse lying on its side in the woods. A rotten smell hung around the animal, but the men could make a meal from it.

Procedures had been ingrained. The prisoners stood for appell; they sometimes got "soup," a clear liquid with a few filthy potatoes; sometimes they scavenged in the forest for wood. The lice were enormous; many people died from typhus and dysentery. Some of the prisoners tried to escape, were caught, and brutally tortured. New prisoners kept arriving every day. When there wasn't room in the barracks, the newcomers slept outdoors. Many weeks passed, and there was still snow on the ground. In these final days of the war, exhausted, half-frozen, and starving, Lev lived in a phantasmagoria that resembled the conditions of plague that the maker of his lost cello had witnessed three hundred years earlier: men lying down anywhere, covered with spots and sores, crying out in fever for help.

"Until the last minute," the Germans chose to remain in the camp. Finally orders were sent down for another evacuation. This time Lev and six of his friends, including Shelkan, decided to disobey. They remembered the horrors of the previous march, the sight of hundreds of frozen bodies shot and left in the ditches. They knew in their weakened condition that chances of survival were slim. In the morning they didn't appear at roll call. They hid beneath their barracks, lying on their stomachs. When enough time had passed they drew lots to see who would go out, look around, and make sure the Germans were gone. After a while the two lookouts returned with reassurances. Then in exhaustion they all fell asleep.

DEATH OF JACOB SCHORR

The next day, March 10, 1945, they woke in silence, stumbling off their "shelves," onto the dirt floor. They stood for a moment in the barrack, disoriented and hungry. One of them opened the door and the others followed him outside. To their surprise they saw more prisoners wandering through the camp. There were no guards. For the first time in many years they were on their own. Lev's group dispatched Jacob Schorr to the camp kitchen. He had always demonstrated talent for finding food. Some of the others climbed to the top of the hill, where they had a view of the pine forest and the road leading to the small city of Lauenburg.

What they saw horrified them. A line of tanks was moving slowly in their direction. The vehicles were far away, each one appearing no bigger than a grain of sand, but the prisoners assumed these were German tanks defending the Pomeranian countryside, coming to take back the camp. Everyone was in despair, running in panic in all directions. Lev, with a small group of friends, fled to the woods.

In the excitement they hardly noticed one of their guards dressed in prison clothes and lying on the forest floor. The men looked at one another. The guard, "an elderly Volksturmer," asked, "What are you doing here?" He assessed the situation and began to peel off the concentration camp clothes he was disguised in. Sitting beneath a tree, he pulled up the pants of his German uniform. With the change of clothing he regained his authority. "Now you'll see the power of the Führer!"

But the prisoners heard the faint shouting in the distance, "*Tovarischi!*"—"Comrades!" Suddenly they realized the tanks belonged to Soviets.

The shelling was getting closer and louder, and the tanks were targeting Gotentov, firing ahead. There was pandemonium in the camp. Some of the prisoners raced back to the officers' barracks, where they found bed sheets. They ripped them into long, white banners. From the windows they waved them as flags. Several more guards, maybe a half-dozen, now came out of hiding and, with their guns cocked, they began running in the direction of what they thought were German tanks. Many prisoners ran ahead of them, down the hill, trying to escape, and the guards began shooting. Lev was limping and running toward the forest with thirty or forty others. They ran into a grove-like area, and to their astonishment they found Russian soldiers camouflaged in the foliage. The Russians encircled the prisoners, some pointing rifles at them. The soldiers shouted out a barrage of questions, and the prisoners answered as well as they could. Looking at the corpse-like faces, the filth and lice on their torn, striped clothes, the commanding officer sent out orders for the tanks to stop shelling the camp. The Soviets carried some of the prisoners on their tanks as they drove back to the top of the hill. There they found the body of the Austrian Jew, Jacob Schorr, killed from the shell fired into the kitchen.

The Soviets took weapons from the prisoners and their guards. They showed everyone a map: "There are two remaining powers. This is where we are; here are the Americans." Then the first division of Russian soldiers moved out of the camp, but they were followed by thousands of Russian troops, many of the soldiers carrying food and vodka for the freed prisoners. Late in the afternoon, two rickety two-horse carriages came into the gates carrying civilians from the countryside— ragged, bearded men, women covered in shawls. With great excitement they told of atrocities in the villages—executions and rapes. Some of the Germans, trying to escape, were hanged. A Soviet officer instructed the Jews who were listening, "Go into town, find an apartment, and throw the occupants out."

LIBERATED

Lev looked around at the others who were running down the hill. He thought, "I'm liberated," but suddenly his energy was depleted. Before liberation, someone had lanced a boil on his foot. Now he was aware of the pain. He was wheezing in the cold. He dragged himself past the barracks where the *muselmen*, those who had given up on life, had slept. There were a few dead bodies. Some had perished in the excitement of the day. He hobbled to the gate of the camp. There was a Jewish boy, a survivor whom the others had "pulled through." The child spoke Russian poorly. Some of the soldiers were mimicking his mistakes with Jewish gestures. Lev was disgusted by his liberators.

In the distance he could see fire engulfing the provincial towns. Suddenly he was anxious. He asked himself, "Tomorrow, where will I get another piece of bread?" Instead of going out through the camp gates, he turned around. He limped toward the barracks now occupied by German prisoners and Russian guards. It was best to spend another night in the camp, he thought. The Russian soldiers treated him with respect. They shared a meal of salami, bread, and vodka and listened while Lev recounted his story, beginning with the confiscation of his cello.

Chapter 12

Finding an Instrument

SPRING 1945

LAUENBURG

Lev had been without an instrument for four years. Now he was living in the small city of Lauenburg with a group of about fifteen Jewish men and women liberated from Gotentov, "sleeping, cooking, eating together." Germans living in the area had run away, and much of the town had been set on fire by Russian troops. During the first days after liberation, there was a free-for-all, survivors scavenging among the wreckage, taking bread for free off of wagons or from the shops, gathering jellies and marmalade, taking fruits and vegetables from cellars, helping themselves to clothes in the closets of strangers who had abandoned their apartments, and liberating bicycles.

Many of the ex-prisoners developed terrible stomach cramps and some died, having devoured food too quickly. Following that, there was an outbreak of louse-borne typhus, and the survivors became delirious with fever that lasted weeks. In the hospital, Russian officers from the NKVD interrogated the Jews, asking their ages and where they had come from before the war. Later the officers would "come and go from the house." But for a while the survivors were allowed to do as they pleased.

One afternoon, Lev and a friend were walking through the town. When they approached a shop that had a sign in the window, *Konservatorium von Musik*, they decided to go in and look around. Lev was overwhelmed by what he saw. There was an enormous library, volumes of bound scores, bookcases of sheet music and manuscripts. Beneath the cabinets, a variety of musical instruments was arranged on the floor. Almost without thinking, he reached for a cello, lifting it off the floor and between his knees. In the first moments, everything felt completely natural, and then he was suddenly disoriented, realizing it was the first time he had touched a cello in years. The instrument he held was missing two strings, the D and the C. But, with a violin bow that had been lying by his feet, he "got the A string up to pitch." Instinctively, Lev tried to produce sound, pressing the pads of his fingers down on the fingerboard and bowing somehow with the little stick. Just as he applied pressure, an excruciating pain shot through his fingers, and the string cut across his fingertips. He had lost all the calluses that had taken decades to develop. When he attempted less pressure on the fingerboard the tone collapsed into a low *bleep*. The voice in his head said, "I am no longer up to this."

"Try the violin," his friend suggested.

"I can't play a violin." Lev said.

"Well, you can't play that thing either. How about a drum?"

TORUN

Everything in the eastern zone was now controlled by military force. Lev and Gregor Shelkan were interrogated by the NKVD. They were asked what languages they spoke, and they answered: German, Yiddish, Russian, Latvian, French, Italian, and even some English. The Soviets concluded, since they were Jewish and had survived when millions had died, they must be spies who "helped the German machinery." With that, they were transported to Torun, a city in north-central Poland with medieval forts and a camp that had housed British POWs before liberation. The German facility was now effectively converted to a Soviet internment camp where refugees from Eastern Europe and the Baltic states were being collected and prepared for repatriation.

The entrance to the camp was a crude wooden gate, and inside there were many long, shed-like buildings. Lev was a prisoner again for many months, and his spirit was broken. Then he was appointed director of the camp theater, and things became somewhat better. One day, in passing, he told his commanding officer that since he was a cellist, he'd like to get hold of a cello. The officer was curious. He said he'd do what he could to locate an instrument. Not long after that he told Lev that he'd found one. Together they left the camp in a horse-drawn cart, "with a sixteen-year-old boy leading the horse." The boy led them to a house on the outskirts of the city and, inside, they saw a cello, "a beaten-up, box of a thing," three-quarter-sized. The endpin was missing. They took the instrument and a bow, loaded them on the cart, and returned to the camp.

The officer was delighted with himself. Walking through the camp gate, he shouted for everyone to hear, "I've got a cello!" Then he took Lev to the camp captain, who said, "Play for me, play *Temnaya Noch* [The Dark Night]." This had been a popular Soviet song from the war: "The dark night separates us . . . I have faith in you . . . That faith has shielded me from bullets in the dark night . . ." Lev only half-knew the piece but realized if he wanted to keep the cello he'd have to play it. He sat down. Since the cello didn't have an endpin, he squeezed it between his bent knees and "attempted the song." While he was playing, he was thinking, "Perhaps it will be okay, maybe I can regain something here." But while he was concentrating on technique, the cello dropped from his knees onto the ground.

"What's happened?" asked the officer.

Lev gestured that the endpin was missing.

"Stay where you are!" The officer ran off. In a minute he came back with a log and then, ingeniously, he whittled it to fit in an endpin hole.

SING, NACHTIGALL

With the aid of an "inattentive Polish officer," an officer who had invited them to his house to play checkers, Lev and Gregor Shelkan "slipped" away from the camp. Lev left the cello behind—"When you escape, it's difficult to take a cello with you."

Their goal was to reach Berlin before Soviet authorities could catch up with them. They traveled by train and on foot, following side roads through forests and muddy farmland with apple and plum orchards. Between the villages and demolished cities, they encountered caravans of other stragglers, refugees, and vagabonds walking through the rubble of incinerated tanks, planes, and spilled ammunition, holding tightly to their satchels and old leather suitcases. They lined up in railway stations and churches for bread and soup, turnips, eggs, coffee, a mug of beer, milk, or water from the pumps. In the towns where travelers had to register with identity cards, they feared the Russians would make trouble, but sometimes they took extra time to view their surroundings.

One day they were in a small city in Upper Silesia, and Lev saw a cello through the glass in a music shop. Though Shelkan was hesitant, they went inside to look around. Lev couldn't resist picking up the instrument. This one was entirely different from the crude box of wood in Torun. It was "clean," in good repair, and had a decent coat of varnish. Lev began to play, and the shopkeeper came by to listen. "I'll give you a special price on the cello," he said, and then he asked Lev to play "his favorite song": "*Sing, Nachtigall, Sing. Ein Lied aus alten Zeiten. . . .*"

Again, it was a well-known, melancholy song, made popular in wartime German cinema: "Sing a song from the old times . . . Bring back happiness. . . ." Lev began to play. But part way through he paused, revolted by "the piece of meaningless nonsense."

"I don't like this cello!" he said, and they left the shop.

EARLY SPRING 1946

LIEGNITZ

The two musicians continued going west, sleeping on the street, in barracks, and in barn stalls. Years later Lev would marvel at how they burned bags of old reichsmarks to keep themselves warm. They still had the "satisfactory" clothes they snatched after liberation and the prisoner jackets from Stutthof, which they kept in a sack. When it was feasible they squeezed onto trains, traveling from one half-destroyed station to the next, the cars "literally covered inside and out with human beings."

Finally they reached Liegnitz, *Legnica*. At the station, Lev noted, "there were still too many Russians about." Like so many other cities, Liegnitz, which had once been known for its mulberry and chestnut trees, Baroque-era churches, and academies, was now filled with the burnt vestiges of village houses, windowless brick walls, and hills of debris. Tens of thousands of war wounded had been deported there after the fighting was over, and the town had been converted to a massive army hospital. Then it was separated into zones for the Soviets, Poles, and remaining Germans.

Under the leadership of Marshal Rokossovsky, Legnica was headquarters for the Soviet troops in Poland, the Northern Group of Forces. Handsome, charismatic, and cultured, a "giant"—six foot four—of Polish descent, Rokossovsky had miraculously survived the 1937 purges, and it was said he had a set of metal teeth to prove it. Among his postwar initiatives, Rokossovsky hired actors, dancers, musicians, and a gypsy orchestra to perform in a repertory theater troop. During the day they traveled to local villages and cities, performing for the residents and receiving a small wage. At night they returned to the city where they lived a Bohemian life.

Lev and Shelkan were delighted to be among artists again. Shelkan explained that he had trained in Vienna Conservatory and sang with the opera in Switzerland and Latvia. Immediately he was invited to join the troop, and he registered under the alias of Gregor Raschel, honoring his wife, the violin prodigy, who had died at Rumbula.

For a while, Lev looked on. He was sorry about the instruments he had left behind. Without a cello, he felt useless. Then, reluctantly, he began assisting as an accompanist on the piano and acting in some of the theater sketches. Like Shelkan, he chose an alias: Lew Arnoff-Aramon. The performances were organized in vaudeville style, music and dance alternating with short dramatic numbers. The actors played stock characters: a sad and pining lover, a beautiful woman, "Maria, Maria," a foolish husband (this one was played by Lev). In one of the small towns they had to make do without a piano, and after Shelkan completed his songs, no one clapped. Lev overheard one of the peasants say, "Doesn't he have beautiful hair?"

Among the performers there was a beautiful young woman, a dancer from Poland, a prima ballerina, Nina Bukowska. Nina had studied dance in Poznan with Eugenie Litvinova, who had herself trained in the Imperial School of Ballet along with Nijinsky and Pavlova. Nina was twenty-four years old. During the war, the Nazis had bombed Poznan while she was performing. Her father was injured, and while they were bringing him to the hospital he was caught in more cross fire and shot in the head. Nina saw him die before her eyes. At the end of the war, with her mother who had once sung in the Schumann Theatre in Frankfurt, she left Poznan, traveling south, carrying suitcases of costumes designed for the parts she had choreographed: Spanish, Hindu, and Siamese dances with feathers, golden head-bells, and masks. For Liszt's *Liebestraum* she had a light blue gown—periwinkle—decorated with coral and feathers. Nina had long, dark curls and porcelain-colored skin. She was five foot seven and had lost so much weight during the last days of the war she now weighed 105 pounds. She and Shelkan became friends, and he introduced her to Lev. The dancer and the cellist fell in love.

NINA

The troop—actors, musicians, and dancers—traveled through Silesia, performing for audiences from one small city to the next. Everything was familiar but changed— charred buildings and ragged civilians, bear-like Soviet soldiers guarding the stations and municipal buildings. At night they returned to Liegnitz, and Lev regaled Nina with stories. He told her about Berlin, Leipzig, Paris, and Florence; his travels to Moscow and St. Petersburg; his performances in Barcelona and Oslo, traveling with Mia Slavenska and Joseph Schmidt; his dinner with Baron Edouard de Rothschild. Sometimes he would describe the camps, his sister delirious from typhus, the female guard beating Gerda until she ran away. He would talk about the smallest things he remembered, the lice he saw on the blanket a Hungarian woman carried across her shoulders or the bright sound of his beautiful cello, the cello that had been confiscated, its deep and fluid voice, the way it would shift registers with absolute clarity. Every note had been vivid and full of color. Nina would listen all night, filled with compassion. When Lev talked to her he also seemed to come alive.

A PYRAMID OF DIRT

One evening the traveling entertainers were performing in Liegnitz for Rokossovsky and the Soviet troops. While Lev was backstage, he noticed a Russian officer whose face seemed familiar. He looked again and realized the officer was a friend from Riga. He and Lev embraced, both of them feeling as though they had encountered a ghost. Formerly in charge of military entertainment, the Russian officer had recently been promoted to a position where he was overseeing the storage, distribution, and shipment of "liberated" materials. Lev explained how desperately he wanted a cello. His friend said he'd help.

The following day the officer brought Lev to an enormous warehouse that was stocked with clothes, hats, lamps, chairs, curtains, crystal, and cutlery. They walked among tables of goods, inspecting harmonicas, shoes, cooking pots, and sagging accordions, until finally they came to a gigantic pile of dirt filled with rubbish, a kind of "pyramid." From the middle of this heap, Lev thought he recognized the neck and scroll of a cello. They pulled the body of the instrument out and shook it off. Lev could hardly believe his eyes. The instrument must have been covered in dirt during the entire war. It had no bridge or tuning pegs, strings, or varnish—"it was a naked cello." His friend was delighted with himself. The next day, he said, they would have it restored.

CHANSON TRISTE

They entered an instrument shop that specialized in guitars and balalaikas. The officer walked over to the luthier and began telling him Lev's story, starting with his studies with Piatigorsky in Berlin, the concerts he had given in Madrid and Rome, his friendship with Joseph Schmidt, his recordings for radio, the Amati, the Neuner, two bows, a Tourte, and a Lamy. He told him how Lev had spent years as a slave laborer in Riga and how he was deported in the cargo hold of a ship, "packed like herring in a barrel." He described Stutthof, the death of Lev's sister, and Burggraben, the camp that had no water, and the forced march through ice-glazed forests.

The balalaika maker was overcome with sympathy: "I'm sure I can fix this cello and have it ready in a week."

A week later, Lev returned to the shop but looked with horror at the cello. The bridge was now a block of wood with an arch scooped from the center. Balalaika strings knotted together stretched from tuning pegs to the tailpiece. Still there was no C string. The luthier stepped forward: "I was so affected by your story, I painted the cello." With that final touch, Lev used to say, "the instrument had no vibration in the slightest."

Not wanting to hurt the fellow's feelings, Lev thanked him and fled the shop, returning to his old friend in despair. Still, the officer from Riga was undiscouraged: "Wait and see, I'll find another one," he said. And within a few days he produced a second instrument, a cello of slightly better quality, although it also was missing a string.

Then Lev was informed he was expected to play the cello in concert. His officer friend wanted to hear his favorite "song," Tchaikovsky's *Chanson Triste*. "He called it a song, I call it a piece," Lev would say. Again, the melody had become popular during the war when Zarah Leander recorded it in Germany and Eva Busch sang it in occupied France, "*chaque jour mon coeur n'appellait. . . .*" Lev tried to prepare for the performance, concentrating on producing sound for the beautiful and melancholic composition, but when he went onstage with his ragged costume and poor cello and the pianist started to improvise an accompaniment, a small child began to giggle, and laughter caught hold of the full audience.

TCHAIKOVSKY TRIO

He wanted to throw out the cello, give up music altogether, but with Nina's encouragement Lev kept at it and practiced. "Do I sound all right? What does it sound like?" he would ask constantly. With a pianist and a violinist among the Soviet soldiers, he formed a trio, and after some rehearsing they began performing together.

One day they were invited to play in Waldenberg, a small city at the foot of a ring of mountains. The town had a huge theater with 2,500 seats. When the entertainers arrived, the hall was full and people were even standing in the back and in the aisles. The musicians were bewildered by the crowd but went on stage and began playing the Tchaikovsky Trio. The music brought back memories of the evenings in Italy with Mrs. Daliba Jones and the performances in the Riga ghetto and at Lenta, which broke so many hearts. But the audience in Waldenberg was different; they were shuffling their feet, whispering to one another, and moving about in their chairs. Little by little they left their seats until, at the end, there were only a few dozen listeners remaining. During intermission Lev asked what was going on. Everyone, he was told, had come to hear the Red Army Chorus and Dance Ensemble, which had canceled at the last minute.

The following day Lev was called in by a Soviet officer who happened to be Jewish. The man spoke to him in a familiar code: "We think it's time for you to go home now."

Lev understood. Not long before this, a group of Russian soldiers had forcibly entered the apartment of one of the other entertainers, a singer, and taken her away. The officer nodded. "Tomorrow a comrade will come for you. He'll take you to repatriation camp about twenty-four kilometers to the north. From there you'll return to Russia."

4 MAY 1946

ESCAPE

Lev told Shelkan and Nina he planned to escape. He had heard that Lodz had become a transit point for Jews from Poland and the Baltic states and a headquarters for *Bricha*, an organization which was helping people get to Palestine and the West. If Lev managed to arrive there safely he'd send a message. "If you don't hear, forget it."

The next morning, the Soviet officer arrived at Lev's apartment, and together they walked to the railroad. Lev had a sack of clothes, his papers, and some money he'd earned from entertaining. He didn't bring his cello but, among his belongings, he carried a picture of Nina dancing *Liebestraum*. A wreath of flowers crowned her hair and she wore an organdy gown. Balanced on point, she let her slender right hand trail behind and to her side. On the back, she had written: "*In ein Gewebe wanden die Gotter Freud und Schmerz. Sie webten und erfanden ein armes Menschenherz*"—"The gods wound joy and pain into a fabric and from this they wove and invented the poor human heart."

The two of them, Lev and the officer, stood on the platform together. As the train was approaching, he received instructions: "You won't need a ticket. When you disembark, another comrade will be waiting. He'll take you to the camp."

Miraculously, the officer went into the station just as two trains were coming into the station from opposite directions. Without his minder, Lev looked carefully and determined that one was headed toward Breslau. In an instant he made the calculation that Breslau wasn't on the route to the Soviet camp. He climbed on board, and what happened next was like a fairy tale. A gypsy woman was sitting in his train compartment. In her hand, she held a deck of cards. "Would you like to hear your fortune?" She dealt Lev his cards. "I see you've got troubles. Water and adversity stand before you. Perhaps, you'll overcome. . . ."

LODZ

That night Lev slept in the station at Breslau and, the next day, he shoved his way onto a train headed for Lodz. When he disembarked, Lev could see crowds of Jewish refugees in the streets. Messages were posted on walls of buildings, names of the missing and those who were mourned. The Lodz Jewish Committee had established an information center where people could register. The Joint Distribution Committee had begun to set up orphanages and schools. Administrators were taking testimony from child survivors and others who had stories to tell. Lev had heard that the Jewish underground was providing identification papers, traveling money, and living arrangements for those who wanted to leave Eastern Europe. He had a contact, a man who had been a major in the Polish resistance army during the war. From the "major" he was sent to Willy Dym, businessman, bookkeeper, metal novelties manufacturer, photographer, mandolin player, and amateur cellist. Willy Dym and his wife, Helli, took Lev into their home and sent instructions to Nina and Gregor Shelkan.

BURIED CELLO

There's an interesting story about Willy Dym. During the war he had worked as a slave laborer in a lumber mill near Lvov. Before that, at the beginning of German occupation, he had given whatever was valuable, his cameras and photographs, some watches, and a few pieces of family silver, to a Christian acquaintance for safekeeping. Among Willy's possessions there had also been a cello. After a while, his non-Jewish friend became nervous about the instrument, too large to conceal should German authorities come visiting. Reluctant to endanger his family because of his association with a Jew, he wrapped the cello and cello case in oilcloth and buried it in the ground.

When Lev heard this he convinced Willy they should retrieve the instrument. Together they made the trip into the countryside, walking on roads still littered with rubble and sand, past the ruins of ramshackle houses, until they reached the deserted outbuilding that had belonged to the Christian friend. In a shack filled with burlap sacks and barrels, they quietly searched for a shovel and carried it into a muddy meadow. They paced off from the fir tree once used as a marker. Six or seven feet in one direction and then in another. They dug a few holes in the soft ground and almost gave up. Then, half-stooped over a pile of earth, one of them hit an object with the shovel. They dug around it. Wedging the shovel underneath, they lifted up a cello case wrapped in oilcloth. The case was almost completely rotten, but the cello was intact. In another version, the cello had decomposed.

EARLY SUMMER 1946

BERLIN

Shelkan and Nina also escaped from Liegnitz. Shelkan followed the same route as Lev, but Nina and her mother went through Czechoslovakia and Austria before making their way to Munich. From Lodz, Lev and Shelkan traveled to Warsaw. Everywhere they looked there were mountains of broken cement and stone, bomb craters, buildings without roofs, and iron gates crumpled in the debris. On the outskirts they witnessed the surreal market scene described by Czeslaw Milosz: "Soviet girls, blouses bulging with their heavy breasts, were directing traffic: military trucks, jeeps, rusty cars which used to be taxis, rickshaws, handcarts. The crowd: Soviet infantrymen, tank crews, NKVD men, women in shawls . . . with rucksacks, shabby civilians with bundles, Polish soldiers—everybody milling about, buying and selling shirts, tires, canned goods, rolls of cloth, vodka, accordions, trousers, radios, half-burned books. . . ."

From their Warsaw contact they were directed to the Russian sector of Berlin. Like everyone else, the two musicians went to Brandenburger Tor, Berlin's thriving black market, where anything on earth could be traded from saddle bags or open lorries. The most basic currency in Berlin was cigarettes. Journalists joked that butts collected off the ground were considered "legal tender." Russian soldiers with money in their pockets were looking for wristwatches, and many of them strapped several upon their arms at one time. Lev and Shelkan hoped to sell their services as interpreters "or anything else."

Near the old gate they noticed a "tall American officer" who was speaking "perfect Russian" to a Soviet officer. Cautiously, after the Soviet officer had moved on, Lev stepped toward the American but whispered in Russian, "I'd like to talk to you." The American gestured for him to wait for a moment. He disappeared and then returned in a jeep, motioning them to jump in.

They drove over the line in the jeep—at last, Lev had made "the complete circle," from the mecca of Berlin in the late twenties to the safe haven of the American sector.

JULY 1946
BERLIN

Again the Jewish musicians were interrogated. But this time they were released to become "guests" of the American intelligence officer, Nelson Chipchin. For a while they were part of the underground economy, Chipchin providing them with "suits, bicycles, and coffee." In return they sold cigarettes in the DP camps, "bringing the proceeds back to him." In Berlin, news about acquaintances traveled by word of mouth, from friend to friend. Some of the survivors from Lenta (they called themselves "*Die Strickerli*," the knitters, since they had worked the machines in Riga) had also made it to Germany. Through *Die Strickerli*, Lev heard that Karl Westen, the former concertmaster who had been so loyal during the days of the Riga Ghetto, was in a camp in Hamburg. Lev wanted badly to see him, and the American intelligence officer arranged an interzone pass so Lev could cross into the French and then the British sector. Lev made his connection with another intelligence officer, a man "dressed in mufti" and, through him, managed a reunion with his old friend to thank him.

DAILY LIFE IN BERLIN

The joy of freedom became less and less. Why? Because life went on its way and every human being has new problems every day... no shirts, no socks, no razors....

Daily life in Berlin was oddly surreal. Lev and Shelkan stole some window frames. Their barracks in the DP camp didn't have windows, and when they saw a stack of frames lying on the ground, they decided to take matters into their own hands. While they were hauling them over their shoulders they were detected by a Jewish policeman and sent to the director of the UNRRA camps in Berlin, who was only half-amused. *"Du hast mein windows gestolen?"* he asked. But he also took an interest in the two musicians.

Lev and Shelkan began to collaborate in a new way. Shelkan wrote Yiddish poetry, and Lev adapted the poems into lyrics for simple compositions he was writing. The scores incorporated Hebrew-sounding melodies. Their first piece, *Der durchgematerter Weg*, *The Road Full of Torment*, commemorated life in the camps and their losses. The music was published for distribution in the DP camps, and on the cover Lev and Shelkan posed in their prison jackets with ascots around their necks.

One day, on the street, Lev noticed another American whose face looked familiar. It puzzled him but he couldn't place it. He walked ahead, into his barracks, and up a flight of stairs. Suddenly he realized he had been looking at a school friend from Riga whose family had emigrated to America before the war. He ran downstairs and stood in front of the officer. "Who are you?" he asked, and suddenly they embraced.

His friend was the officer in charge of the entire Berlin PX and, through him, Lev got an apartment, a telephone, and a cello—an "unbelievable" instrument with a beautiful, robust tone. Lev thought, "This would be a joy to play for the rest of my life." The sweet-sounding instrument had been built by Francesco Ruggieri, a violin maker who was born in an outlying neighborhood of Cremona when Nicolò Amati was crafting instruments for dukes and kings. Like Amati, he lived through the times of famine and plague. Experts say that Ruggieri's very beautiful cellos, slightly smaller than the standard of the time, were influenced by Amati's "mathematically derived" forms, and even in his lifetime they were played by professional musicians who admired the purity and depth of their sound.

With the Ruggieri in hand, Lev returned to the arduous work of rebuilding technique, teaching himself what he had internalized long ago from his studies with Klengel, von Glehn, and Piatigorsky. Now his plans were becoming more concrete. He would use his time in Berlin to reconstitute his technique. He obtained documents from Klindworth-Scharwenka. He applied to the American consulate for permission to emigrate. Filled with optimism, he began a series of compositions, *Jewish Pictures for Orchestra: Jewish Wedding, Learning the Talmud, Rachel at the Well, Hassidim Are Dancing*. In the back of his mind, he was thinking about Nina. He had news that she and her mother had arrived in Munich. He began to think he could reestablish himself as a musician and marry her.

MARRIAGE

Lev "made a furtive trip to Munich" to bring Nina and her mother to Berlin. Nina's teacher, Eugenie Litvinova, was teaching in Berlin and Nina was overjoyed to be reunited with her. In December, Nina, Lev, and Shelkan performed together at the Tivoli Theater in the Tempelhof DP camp accompanied by William Otto. The concert began with Massenet's "Elegy," Lev playing the cello and Shelkan singing the art song with its famous refrain:

> *Comme en mon coeur tout est sombre et glacé !*
> *Tout est flétri*
> *pour toujours !*

The longing and wistful sound of the melody, the aching sadness of the text—*all is withered forever*—must have reflected the mood that would descend precipitously upon Lev in those years. Through her choreography, merging classical ballet with expressive pantomime, Nina constructed a loving response, performing Sibelius's *Valse Trieste*. On February 15, 1947, they were married in a civil service in Berlin.

CONCERTS

Late in February Lev was invited to tour for ten days with Michael Taube and other musicians. Taube had once conducted the Berlin State Opera and was now leading the Palestine Philharmonic, known for its string section, violinists and cellists from Eastern and Central Europe, whose performances were "little short of perfection." They gave concerts at DP camps in Germany and Austria, and the experience stirred up a lot of emotion. Lev was excruciatingly aware of how many years he had lost, and he wanted to separate himself from the hopelessness he saw in so many of the Jewish faces, but, later in the year, he toured again: "I played for the people from the steamship *Exodus* who lived in the hope of going to Palestine." In the recitals he often performed *Rachel at the Well* which Nina danced to. He chose Rachel rather than Rebecca, he said, because Rachel's life had been "filled with tragedy and sorrow..."

OLD MAN STROBEL

Life with Nina was difficult in the small apartment they shared with her mother and Shelkan. One day Lev's friend from Riga, the American officer in charge of the PX, came with bad news. His wife wanted the Ruggieri. She said they could sell it on the black market and make an enormous profit.

Lev was devastated, but again he was determined to find a good instrument. This time he turned to "Old Man Strobel," a dealer he knew from his student days in Berlin. Strobel listened to Lev's story, beginning with the confiscation of the Amati. He described the years in the Riga Ghetto, the camps, the cello without an endpin, his escape from the Soviets, the troupe in Liegnitz, the "naked cello" he found in the "pyramid" of dirt, and the cello he played in front of Rossokovsky. He described his second escape from the Soviets and Willy Dym, his journey through Poland, the intelligence agent who took him into the American zone, his friend in the PX, and the Ruggieri—a beautiful instrument he had imagined playing for the rest of his life. Strobel listened to it all and said he wanted to help, but many valuable instruments had perished in the bombings over Germany. Everyone was talking about Walter Hamma from Stuttgart, the most famous violin dealer in Germany, who had put his finest instruments in his underground safe. After the allied bombing raids, his house was destroyed and, days later, when he returned to the cellar and opened the safe he found the heat of the bombs had turned the violins to charcoal. Strobel also had his own interesting story.

Before the Soviet army entered Berlin he had placed a Stradivarius cello in a casket and buried it in a field. He told Lev he could have the Strad if he would help dig it up.

The next evening Lev assembled fifteen boys with shovels from the DP camp. They followed Strobel and his son into the Russian zone, far into the countryside. It was dangerous to be there; everyone knew if they were detected by the Soviets they'd be arrested instantly. Strobel stood in the center of a field. "This is the place," he said. Then, "I think it's here, in this spot." But when they dug for a while and didn't find anything, he changed his mind, "No, dig over here." And then, "No, not here, over there." The field was vast. "Where was it, where was it?" he asked himself. "I forget." He kept changing his mind. In the darkness, Old Man Strobel stood in the middle of the field, chain-smoking, "a little cigarette hanging from the corner of his mouth." What they were doing was totally illegal, and Strobel never could remember where he had planted the casket with the Stradivarius. They went on digging all night.

APRIL 10, 1948

NEW YORK

With a feather in her hat, fur jacket, black pants, and black pumps obtained from relief organizations, Nina carried one cello case in her left hand and the other under her right arm as she walked off the gangplank of the SS *Marine Marlin*, which had sailed from Bremen on March

29. Through Old Man Strobel and his friend in the PX, Lev had acquired two mediocre instruments, not much more than wooden boxes. The crossing had been filled with emotion. In his youth Lev had imagined making the trip to America with the fanfare of an accomplished soloist. Later, during the war years, it became a fantastic, unattainable dream. On shipboard, with only a few dollars in his pocket, Lev began to measure his dream against reality. On the one hand, it was a miracle to be alive, traveling to a new life with a beautiful young wife. On the other hand, he was depleted, humiliated by his refugee status, and frightened about the future.

In New York, dependent upon United Services for New Americans, the Jewish agency that provided an allowance, arranged housing, and scouted for employment, Lev was frustrated. When he was told he would be evaluated by the Vocational Adjustment Division, he became irate. That was when he raised his voice, grabbed a paperweight off a desk, and threatened to throw it through the glass window unless the caseworker agreed to contact his teacher, Piatigorsky.

Immediately upon receiving Lev's phone call, Piatigorsky boarded a train from Philadelphia, arriving at the Windsor Hotel in New York a few hours later with newspaper reporters and cameras from the *Herald Tribune* and the *New York Times*. The next day headlines read: "Piatigorsky Has Joyful Reunion with Cello Pupil Held by Nazis" and "Piatigorsky, Pupil Meet After 9 Years."

Once again Lev was leading an enchanted life. Piatigorsky took Lev and Nina to the Copacabana. He promised to do what he could to find his pupil a position in the American music world. He brought him a cello, a cello case, and a bow. The cello made by Honoré Derazey in Mirecourt in the mid-nineteenth century was a "decent instrument," superior to the wooden boxes he had acquired in Germany. But that wasn't the end of Lev's difficulties. America was inundated with musical celebrities, refugees from Europe, and Piatigorsky warned, "In America they don't want serious music." To make matters worse, Lev, at thirty-six, was old for entrance into an orchestra. He was soon in the office of a new caseworker whose report reflected exasperation. Lev was unwilling to consider employment without consulting Mr. Piatigorsky. When he was asked what exactly Mr. Piatigorsky could do, Lev refused to answer. The caseworker expected him "to get started immediately," but Lev needed time to practice for auditions. When he "discussed with Mr. A. the fact that he might not have as much status here as a musician that he had in Europe," he hit a raw nerve.

Lev and Nina practiced night and day, and there were complaints at the hotel about noise they made. People knocked on the walls and yelled across the airshaft, "Stop the cellist and ballet dancer! Close your windows!" When the agency required they move to other lodgings, they moved from the Hotel Belleclaire to the Marseilles; it seemed impossible to find a suitable apartment. Just when rooms came available, both Nina and Lev became ill. After only a few days in their new residence, the landlady turned them out and refused to relinquish their deposit. In the residence hotel, Nina wanted to cook, but they had no utensils. She became worried about her mother, who remained in Germany. Lev was restless and nervous. He couldn't tolerate being alone. He drank too much. And there was the matter of the musician's union, which required a fifty-four-dollar initiation fee and six months' residency in the United States.

Piatigorsky arranged auditions, radio broadcasts, and introductions to other musicians. After a few months, two offers came in—the first with Kansas City, under the baton of Hans Schweiger, and the second with the Dallas Symphony, an orchestra that had stopped performing during the war and was being rebuilt by the Hungarian-born conductor Antal Dorati.

Lev had auditioned for Lester Salomon from the Dallas orchestra while Dorati was in Europe. Afterward, Dorati came to New York to talk with Lev, who was losing confidence. Dorati and Lev sat on benches facing Central Park West. Lev said he worried he wasn't up for the job; during the war "his nerves had been shot." Dorati "understood things without being told." He reassured Lev. He wanted him to be assistant principal cellist. Janos Starker, who was coming from Europe, would share the first chair.

After negotiations with the union, Lev signed a contract with the Dallas Symphony, but still he was uneasy. One day he carried his cello into the offices of the Jewish agency. "The cello," he said, "was difficult to play. . . . It was not a very good one." He said that his friends thought he'd have a better chance in America if he had a better instrument, one that could produce a better tone. Someone had offered him a famous instrument for fifteen hundred dollars, a cello that had been made by Carlo Tononi. The caseworker reminded him he had been hired on the basis of his performance with his current cello. Lev said he was afraid "*in the future* he would not be able to further his career unless he had a new cello." His friend, he said, "had a deep understanding of my suffering and troubles." The caseworker suggested that he arrange a loan. Lev said the burden would be too much. The caseworker looked at the Derazey and made a counteroffer: he agreed to pay for the repair of fifteen to twenty dollars on "the not very good" instrument. Lev said before the war he had a wonderful Amati that had been taken from him.

Epilogue

Lev played the Derazey until 1959, when a Dallas businessman and art collector, Clarence Draggert, purchased a group of Stradivarius instruments for the Dallas Symphony. The cello, the Delphino/Markevitch, had well-documented provenance beginning in 1712: "About three years after the instrument was finished on[e] M. Delphin, a man of some attainments, but not a musician, bought with all its contents a house in Cremona. Here among other valuables, he found the Stradivarius cello . . ." Named for its first known owner as well as a more recent one, Andrei Markevitch, who had been an amateur musician and senator in Tsarist Russia, the instrument had been smuggled to Hill & Sons in London at the time of the Revolution and civil war. There are newspaper clippings of Lev with the majestic instrument and the caption: "One of the rare specimens of famed Stradivarius cellos from the 'Golden Period.'" But he played it only a few years before his patron took it back. With a heavy heart Lev turned again to Piatigorsky, who helped him finance his beloved Goffriller, the cello he played to the end of his life.

Lev's identification with his instruments was deep, and he never forgot the loss of the Amati. He sometimes talked about his "old colleague," the man who had confiscated it in 1941. Had he kept it for himself, Lev wondered? In 1944, at just about the time Lev and the few survivors of the Riga Ghetto worked as longshoremen, loading the last German steamers at Riga Harbor, most of the musicians from the Latvian Radio Orchestra were being evacuated to Germany. Had they stayed in Riga, the Soviets would have treated them as collaborators. Lev knew where "his colleague" lived in Germany after the war, the university where he taught, and who his students were. The two were almost exactly the same age, and the music world was small.

Did his old colleague play the Amati during the war? Did he carry it with him when he was evacuated from Riga? Did the instrument change hands in Latvia or Germany? Is someone playing it today? When I spoke to Willem de Vries, an expert on musical instruments and manuscripts plundered by the Nazis, he explained how difficult it is to know the answers. Most of the documents from Riga were sent to Ratibor (Silesia) in 1943. In 1945 they were confiscated when the Red Army arrived. Today they could be anywhere in Russia, "but no Russian archive will tell you that freely; it is still 'loot from the enemy.'" He added, "The Rosenberg commandos [Einsatzstab Reichsleiter Rosenberg (ERR)] did far more invisible plundering in Eastern Europe than in the West. Infrastructures and communications in the East were much less sophisticated. You could easily confiscate a museum, music shop, or music collection in, for example, Latvia without the whole country or the authorities noticing. You did not get a receipt from the ERR when they took your violin. They did not always document their confiscations. Valuable instruments were sent to Berlin with perhaps only a list of contents, no names of owners, circumstances, or places. And in 1943 the majority of Sonderstab Musik [the command force responsible for confiscations having to do with music] documents were burned in Berlin during an air raid. . . ." What Lev couldn't have known is that a much younger cellist with the same surname as his old "colleague" is a professional cellist in Germany today.

Amnon Weinstein, an Israeli violin maker, collects and restores instruments that belonged to Jews at the time of the Holocaust, "silent witnesses." He's donated several to Yad Vashem, the Holocaust Martyrs' and Heroes' Remembrance Authority. One of his instruments is a violin attributed to Yaakov Zimmerman, a Jewish luthier who worked in Warsaw in the 1920s. On the front of the violin there are five inlaid stars of David and a large one decorates the back. Weinstein and his son purchased the violin from a woman in Florida. He talks about himself as a detective: "I can definitely say that this violin was played on in the worst conditions—snow, rain, wind. This is why the varnish is completely destroyed on the top, while on the back the varnish is almost in mint condition." When I spoke to Mr. Weinstein, we talked about the fate of "Jewish" instruments (a piano was thrown from a window in Dresden)—mandolins, violins, and violas that had come from all over Europe. Some had been warehoused in the synagogues in Prague like ghosts of their owners.

Mr. Weinstein is also an expert on Amatis, and he was interested in Lev Aronson's story. Though it would be difficult to prove ownership, he thought I should find out more about the cellist with the last name of Lev's old colleague; he might know something. The idea intrigued me, and for a while I played with it in my mind. One day, by accident, I heard a recording by the chamber group I know the young cellist performs with. Their sound was bright but deep. They played together with simplicity and beauty. I remembered Lev's struggles and his devotion to the music. I thought about the young musician and the conversation we might have. I put the idea aside.

There's a website, Cozio.com, that provides news, forums, photographs, and documentation on fine, old string instruments. I've searched the database periodically, wondering if Lev's Amati could be identified there. Currently Cozio shows twelve cellos made by Nicolò Amati. Some can be disqualified easily—the Nicolaus Amatus Cremonen with a mother-of-pearl inscription of the Medici coat of arms decorating its fingerboard or the 1650 Amati that has been in the Russian State Collection since 1920. Leonard Rose owned the Grand Amati, dated 1662. Musicians have an intimate knowledge of their instruments, from the chisel marks to the sound. Lev would have known if Rose had been playing his cello. Some of the instruments have been archived at the Smithsonian, which holds the Jacques Français Collection, certificates and photographs of instruments that had passed through his shop or had been handled by Emil Herrmann, who had shops in Berlin and New York.

A connoisseur can tell a lot by studying photographs, studying the scrolls or wood patterns as they show up in the play of light, for instance. But I'm not a connoisseur. I emailed photographs of Lev Aronson's cello from the 1930s to the website. The publisher could not find a clear match with the catalogued ones.

One night at dinner I mentioned Lev Aronson's story to a German historian who has worked for several years in the field of cultural property and law. Wolfgang, who has both a judicious and inventive mind, was attentive to the details. When I finished my story he made an interesting suggestion. Perhaps it would be useful, he said, simply to place an article in a German newspaper or journal and see what comes of it. Perhaps it would catch the attention of someone who knows about the instrument, about its fate. It should begin: "My name is Lev Aronson. . . . Born in München-Gladbach of Jewish parents in 1912, I began my musical and cello education at the age of six. . . . I am convinced that somewhere in Germany or Austria someone is playing that priceless Amati cello and Tourte bow. . . ."

Notes

PREFACE

2 *"He enunciated..."* Tim Finholt, "Conversation with Ralph Kirshbaum," *Internet Cello Society*, 1997, http://www.cello.org/Newsletter/Articles/kirshbaum.htm.

2 *"My fate is probably..."* John Ardoin, "Famed cellist Lev Aronson dies at 76," *Dallas Morning News*, 13 November 1988, pp. 33A–34A.

3 *"You couldn't win..."* Conversation with Craig Casper, 23 January 2004.

3 *"That's how it can breathe..."* Conversation with David Caron, 6 January 2004.

LOST CELLO

5 *"I feel so empty and alone..."* Draft of journal entry, *Aronson Uncollected Papers*.

6 *"My name is Lev Aronson..."* Fragments quoted from Lev Aronson's 1986 Letter to FRG, *Aronson Uncollected Papers*.

6 *"fantastic stories of his colorful past"* David Caron, *Erno and Lev*, privately printed.

6 *"Compact bow!"* or *"The train has already left the station!"* Conversation with David Caron, 28 April 2008.

6 *"Show me where in the score..."* Conversation with David Caron, 6 January 2004.

9 *"the typical wide stairs..."* The scene that follows is drawn from Mr. Aronson's detailed account of the confiscation described in his unpublished memoir, *Aronson Uncollected Papers*.

9 *Latvian auxiliary police...* For the role of Latvian paramilitary, see Josifs Steimanis, *History of Latvian Jews*, translated by Helena Belova, revised and edited by Edward Anders (New York: Columbia University Press, East European Monographs, 2002) pp. 128–131 and Andrew Ezergailis, *Latvia: The Missing Center 1941–1944* (Washington, DC: The United States Holocaust Memorial Museum and The Historical Institute of Latvia, 1996), pp. 116–127 and pp. 180–184.

9 *Since Melngalvju nams, the House of Blackheads, was destroyed . . .* Details
   on the destruction of the tower and orchestra's instruments and
   manuscripts: Elmers Zemovics, "75th Anniversary of the Latvian
   National Symphony Orchestra," http://www.music.lv/orchestra/
   history.htm (3 February 2006).

10 *He was accustomed to thinking of himself as "a man of the world". . .*
   Conversation with the violinist Arkady Fomin, 16 June 2008.

FROM JEWISH LIFE

11 *I'm listening to a recording . . . Lev Aronson Plays Cello Classics and
   Encores with Strings, Organ, and Piano: Works by Bach, Handel, Vivaldi,
   Bloch, Couperin,* recorded in 1971 by Lev Aronson with Roger L.
   Keyes (piano) and Joyce Jones (organ), Word WST-8528.

12 *As in much of the Baltic area, the town had been settled . . .* For Mitava
   (Jelgava) history, population figures, and Jewish professions, see
   *Pinkas Hakelhillot Latvia and Estonia: Encyclopedia of Jewish
   Communities, Latvia and Estonia,* edited by Dov Levin (Jerusalem:
   Yad Vashem,1988).

12 *Rastrelli Palace* Draft for autobiography, *Aronson Uncollected Papers.*
   The palace, burned to the ground in 1919, has been reconstructed.

13 *The main synagogue . . .* Postcard: *Mitau, Die Grosse Synagoge.*

13 *"In school there were . . ."* The beautifully detailed description of daily life
   comes from Robert Herzenberg Memoirs Written During the 1940s,
   translated during the 1990s by Leonardo (Leonhard) Herzenberg,
   January 2006, http://www.herzenberg.net/leo/htmlrh/Content.
   html#TofC.

14 *"an unschooled country fiddler . . ."* Details about Lev Aronson's family
   and childhood are contained in Dennis Rooney's interview with Lev
   Aronson, "Free Spirit," *The Strad,* vol. 97 (September 1986) pp.
   338–341.

15 *"Children like him . . . "* Alexander Herzen, quoted from Solo
   Wittmayer Baron, *The Russian Jew under Tsars and Soviets* (London:
   Collier-Macmillan, 1964; New York: Macmillan, 1965), pp. 36–37.
   The story of the conscription of Wulff Aronson is told in Lev
   Aronson's unpublished memoir, *Aronson Uncollected Papers.*

15 *After Wulff's death . . .* Details about Zorach and Pessa Aronson
   in Mitava and Berlin are drawn from biographical notes, *Aronson
   Uncollected Papers.* Professions of parents were indicated on documents
   in Latvijas Valsts Vestures Arhivs.

17 *On April 18, 1915 . . .* There are differing opinions for the exact date of
   departure. Extra time was granted after the Decree of Expulsion was
   issued. See Josifs Steimanis, *History of Latvian Jews,* 24–25 and *The*

Jews of Latvia, ed. M. Bobe, S. Levenberg, I. Maor, and Z. Michaeli (Tel Aviv: Association of Latvian and Estonian Jews in Israel, 1971), pp. 279–282.

17 *Families crowded* ... The expulsion of the Jews of Kurland is described in many memoirs. An especially detailed narrative is contained in "The Autobiography of Solomon Katzen, The Early Years, 1902–1923," http://www.jewishgen.org/Courland/katzen.htm, 24 July 2007.

18 *"sugar, cheese and herring, eggs, boiled meat "* in *Evreiskaia Blagotvoritelnost na Territorii Byvshego SSSR: Stranitsy Istorii* (Jewish Charity on the Territory of the Former USSR: Pages from History), Institut Sotsialnykh I Obshchinykh Rabotnikov; Peterburgskii Evreiskii Universitet (Institute of Social and Community Workers; Petersburg Jewish University), edited by D. Eliashevich and B. Haller. (St. Petersburg, 1998) pp. 100–101.

18 *"As I'm trying to remember... "* Lev Aronson's personal memory of expulsion and life in Voronezh comes from the draft for an autobiography, *Aronson Uncollected Papers.*

19 *Across the mosaic of Eastern European Jewish communities, there were two great traditions....* For a description of Jewish music I'm indebted to Henry Sapoznik's *Klezmer! Jewish Music from Old World to Our World* (New York: Schirmer, 1999) and Mark Slobin's translation and edition of *Old Jewish Folk Music: The Collections and Writings of Moshe Beregovski* (Philadelphia: University of Pennsylvania Press, 1982) which contains the riddle "Do you want to know how many... ?" I've also drawn material from James Loeffler: "Jewish Concert Music," *The YIVO Encyclopedia of Jews in Eastern Europe*, edited by Gershon David Hundert, vol. 2 (New Haven: Yale University Press, 2008), pp. 1228–1233 and *The Most Musical Nation* (New Haven: Yale University Press, forthcoming) as well as Irene Heskes and Arthur Wolfson, *The Historic Contribution of Russian Jewry to Jewish Music* (New York: National Jewish Music Council, 1967).

21 *How were instruments obtained?* Josh Horowitz (Dr. Klez) presented a fine description of klezmer instruments on his website at http://www.budowitz.com. Also, see his comments about Julius Heinrich Zimmerman: Chazzanut Online, Jewish-Music, Re: Boehm &Albert Systems, 28 March 2000, 09.53 (GMT), http://74.125.47.132/sea rch?q=cache:y4CdEkCBDb4J:archive.chazzanut.com/jewish-music/msg01580.html+julius+heinrich+zimmerman+woodwind+shop&hl=en &ct=clnk&cd=2&gl=us&client=safari, 20 January 2009.

21 *"it was coal black ... "* Gregor Piatigorsky, *Cellist* (New York: Doubleday & Company, Inc., 1965), p. 28.

21 *"In Voronezh there was a very rich family... "* Mr Aronson described his introduction to the cello in many places. In this instance I'm

drawing from an oral history interview conducted by Robert Beer, Jewish Historical Society, Dallas, 3 February 1985.

22 *Leo Zeitlin's* Eli Zion . . . The composition, for cello and piano, was first performed at the St. Petersburg Conservatory on 21 April 1913. See Heskes and Wolfson, *The Historic Contribution of Russian Jewry to Jewish Music,* p. 43.

23 *Aron Rafaeovitsch Rubinstein* "The Incredible Story of Lev Aronson, the cellist who was born 'everywhere,'" Olin Chism, *Dallas Times Herald,* 14 January 1979, Sunday, p. 7.

23 *BAI JIDI SPASAI RUSSIA* I've drawn details of the years 1917–1920 from *Lev Aronson,* videocassette, 26 April 1986.

THE STUDENT

25 *"My Dear Levushka . . ."* Piatigorsky letter, 9 February1960, translated by Edward Stankiewicz, *Aronson Uncollected Papers.*

26 *"musical . . . beautiful . . . and full of messages "* From Mr. Aronson's unpublished memoir, *My Remembrances of Piatigorsky, Aronson Uncollected Papers.*

26 *"It's strange; the less I feel I deserve . . ."* Piatigorsky letter, 25 May 1955, translated by Marina Kostalevsky, *Aronson Uncollected Papers.*

27 *"I am very worried about your tour . . ."* Piatigorsky letter, 20 January 1965, translated by Marina Kostalevsky, *Aronson Uncollected Papers.*

27 *"My teenage idol . . ."* See Carolyn Lesh, "Lev Aronson," *The Dallas Morning News,* 2 March 1986, 4E.

27 *Using political connections . . .* Zorach Aronson had known Janis Cakste, Latvia's first president, from before the war, *Lev Aronson,* videocassette, 26 April 1986.

27 *Riga was an elegant city with steeples and spires . . .* Scenes of Riga's parks and streets can be seen in the film "Jewish Life in Prewar Kovno, Riga, and Lvov (prewar footage, home movies of the Katz family in 1929)," USHMM, Story R6-60.4218. Tape 2766.

28 *the Jews, whose population increased . . .* Riga population figures from U.S. Commission and Consular Report: *The Jews of Latvia,* filed between 1920 and 1941, http://www.jewishgen.org/Courland/consular/cons_jews.htm, 14 April 2006.

28 *organized a society of tailors . . .* Zorach Aronson's civic contribution is described in a privately published Yizkor book printed in Latvia, *Aronson Uncollected Papers.*

28 *"took anti-Semitism for granted"* Max Michelson, *City of Life, City of Death* (Boulder: University Press of Colorado, 2004), p. 4.

28 *sang the Jewish chorals . . .* Description of Lev Aronson's parents and

childhood in Riga is drawn from drafts for an autobiography, *Aronson Uncollected Papers*.

30 *Paul Berkowitsch* (Pauls Berkovics). See Ilona Brege, *Cittautu Muziki Latvija, 1401–1939* (Riga: Zinatne, 2001) p. 21 and Bernhard Press, *The Murder of the Jews in Latvia: 1941–1945*, translated by Laimdota Mazzarins (Evanston: Northwestern University Press, 2000) p. 16. According to Mr. Press, Paul Berkowitsch sat in the orchestra beside his cousin, the cardiologist Dr. M. Joffe. He left Riga in the late 1920s and went to Kovno. During the war he lived outside the ghetto with false papers. He learned bookkeeping and survived as an accountant. After the war he became a professor at the Lithuanian Conservatory in Vilnius and was the dean of the conservatory during the last twenty years of his life.

30 *replacing it with a suit jacket* . . . The descriptions of lessons with Paul Berkowitsch and the following years in Berlin and Leipzig are drawn from drafts of Mr. Aronson's *My Remembrances of Piatigorsky, Aronson Uncollected Papers*.

30 *Ivan Suchov* (Ivan Suchow, Ivan Suhovs). Professor at the Riga Conservatory. Later he emigrated to Paris and was the conductor of the Orchestre des ballets du colonel de Basile and professor at Conservatoire Serge Rachmaninov. See Ilona Brege, *Cittautu Muziki Latvija* p. 174.

31 *Mendel Beilis*. See Natem Meir, "Mendel Beilis," *YIVO Encyclopedia of Jews in Eastern Europe* vol. 1, pp. 138–139.

31 *Schwarzbard*. See *Guide to the Papers of Shalom Schwarzbard*, YIVO archives.

35 *Klindworth-Scharwenka*. Lev Aronson's diploma, Bescheinigun, Konservatorium der Muik Klindworth-Scharwenka, reissued 16 December 1946, is contained in *Aronson Uncollected Papers*.

38 *"not a good day for drowning"* Conversation with Evan Drachman, 3 February 2004.

39 *On the sidewalks there were military bands* . . . Scenes of musical activity in the city of Berlin can be seen in the film *Berlin Symphony of a City*, 1927, directed by Walther Ruttman, idea by Karl Mayer, scenerio by Ruttman and Karl Freunk.

39 *"not so much . . . solving immediate problems"* Dennis Rooney, "Free Spirit," *The Strad*.

41 *Artur Schnabel and Albert Einstein were guests* . . . Dr. Jack Frederick Kilpatrick, "Lev Aronson and the Cello are Inseparable Companions," *Dallas Times Herald*, 18 March 1956, G3.

AMATI

42 *"Occupation: Musician . . ."* Carolyn Lesh, "Lev Aronson," *The Dallas Morning News.*

42 *Nicolò Amati.* See Philip Kass, "Nicolò Amati: His Life and Times," *Violin Society of America*, vol. 15, no. 2, pp. 140–198 and "Survival of the Fittest," Carlo Chiesa and Philip Kass, *The Strad*, vol. 107, issue 1280, December 1996, pp. 1296–1301 for an excellent description of the Amati family in Cremona; Marco Vinicio Bissolotti, *The Genius of Violin Making in Cremona* (Cremona: Edizioni Novecento, English edition, September 2000), pp 33–35; Fauso Cacciatori, Bruce Carlson, and Carlo Chiesa, *Il DNA Degli Amati (The Amati's DNA): A Dynasty of Stringed Instrument Makers in Cremona* (Cremona: Ente Triennale Internazionale degli Strumenti ad Arco Consorzio Liutai Antonio Stradivari Cremona, 2006).

43 *Alessandro Manzoni.* For a novelist's description of the plague years, see *The Betrothed* (*I Promessi Sposi*), translated by Archibald Colquhoun (New York: E.P. Dutton & Co., 1951) pp. 531–536.

44 *Luigi Tarisio.* William Alexander Silverman, *The Violin Hunter: The Life Story of Luigi Tarisio, the great collector of violins* (London: W. Reeves, 1957).

45 "Great musicians usually have long relationships with their instruments . . ." Conversation with David Caron, 6 January 2004.

45 *Sonderstab Musik,* Willem de Vries. Author of *Sonderstab Musik: Music Confiscations by the Einsatzstab Reichsleiter Rosenberg under the Nazi Occupation of Western Europe* (Amsterdam: Amsterdam University Press, 1996), documenting the history of Alfred Rosenberg's command force, which confiscated musical instruments, 1940–1945.

45 *Piatigorsky's 1712 Stradivarius:* "Instrument Stolen by Nazis During War: Musician and 1712 Stradivarius Cello Reunited," *New York Times*, 16 January1954.

46 *"Before the war started, I had a wonderful Amati cello . . ."* Lev Aronson letter contained in case file #J-3749, United Services for New Americans. Also see *Lev Aronson Interview*, KYNE TV, Channel 26, Omaha, 11 November 1982. *Lev Aronson* videocassette: ". . . by that time I had a very good instrument."

46 *sable skins.* Diana Rice, "Luxuries that Bring the Highest Prices," *New York Times*, 5 February 1933.

46 *"I asked Carla Shapreau . . . "* Correspondence, 6 July 2006.

48 *Richard Dannler.* Shoah Resource Center, Nuremberg Document NO-5124, Yitzhak Arad, "Plunder of Jewish Property in Nazi Occupied Areas of the Soviet Union," translated by William Templer, Yad Vashem, p. 36, http://www1.yadvashem.org/odot_pdf/Microsoft%20 Word%20-%202277.pdf.

48 *Although he knew the whereabouts . . . Lev Aronson Interview*, KYNE TV.

49 *"a pair of crossed hands . . . "* Details about two trips to Paris are drawn from a draft for an autobiography, *Aronson Uncollected Papers*.

50 *Lovro von Matačić.* The Croatian conductor (1899–1985) began his career in 1919. During his early years, he conducted orchestras in Osijek, Novi Sad, Ljubljana, Belgrade, and Riga. In 1932 he became the conductor of the Zagreb Opera. See Ilona Brege, *Citlautu Muziki Latvia*, p. 121.

50 *"Brownshirts? You know the Spartans. . . "* Details about Lev Aronson's last days in Berlin come from autobiographical notes in *Aronson Uncollected Papers*.

51 *All-Union Music Competition . . .* See Olga Fyodorova, "Russian Musical Highlights of the Twentieth Century, 1933," http://www.vor.ru/century/1933m.html.

51 *"I met the wonderful cellist Knushevitsky . . . "* Sviatoslav Knushevitsky (1901–1974), soloist for the Bolshoi Theater Orchestra and a professor at the Moscow Conservatory, became world famous in David Oistrakh's Trio with Lev Oberin. Description of the All-Union Competition is drawn from autobiographical notes, *Aronson Uncollected Papers*.

51 *Vladimir Shavitch.* For a biographical entry on Shavitch, see Gdal Saleski, *Famous Musicians of a Wandering Race* (New York: Bloch Publishing Co., 1927).

52 *"Synchro-Opera . . ."* *Time Magazine*, 29 March 1937.

52 *"his next stop in Europe"* Details on Italy and other European performances are drawn from drafts for Mr. Aronson's autobiography, *Aronson Uncollected Papers*.

53 *Shavitch's wife, Tina Lerner . . . Grove Dictionary of Music and Musicians*, Sixth Volume (New York: The Macmillan Company,1920).

53 *"sound of his instrumental singing" Lev Arnoff, Violincellist, Management B. Levitas, Riga*, promotional flier, *Aronson Uncollected Papers*.

54 *"beauties in exile"* See Alexandre Vassiliev, *Beauty in Exile: The Artists, Models, and Nobility Who Fled the Russian Revolution and Influenced the World of Fashion* (New York: Henry N. Abrams, 2000).

55 *"young swaggering fellow"* The St. Petersburg audition and following years in Riga are described in "Oral Memoirs of Daniel Arie Sternberg," 12 December 1977– 6 November 1980, Volume 2, Interviews 7–12, The Texas Collection, Baylor University, Waco, Texas, Program for Oral History, pp. 425–431. Mr. Sternberg was the assistant conductor to the Leningrad Philharmonic in the 1930s. He was dean of the Music School at Baylor, 1943–1982.

55 *Victor Babin.* Information about cultural life in Riga in the 1930s

comes from Aronson videocassette, 26 April 1986. Babin (1908–1972) emigrated to the United States in 1938 with his wife, the pianist Vitya Vronsky.

55 *offered first to Latvian musicians with Christian backgrounds.* Conversation with Arkady Fomin, 16 June 2008.

55 *Melngalvju nams.* Program is contained in *Aronson Uncollected Papers.*

56 *"He made four recordings . . ."* Lev Aronson's early recordings are archived in the Fine Arts Division of the Dallas Public Library: Bellaccord-electo, Levs Arnovs pie klavierem Leo Demants. 3653: *Siciliana,* Skumju valsis (Paradis-Caikovskis) *Pec kada sapna* (G. Faure-P. Cazals). 3433: *Barkarolla,* P. Caikovskis *Serenade, E. de Kurtis.* 3232: *Mirstosais Gulbis,* Saint-Saens, *Gavotte,* J.B. Lully. 3265: *Ciganu Melodija,* A. Dvorzaks Austrumu Melodija (Orientale)-CUI.

ON THE VERGE OF WAR

57 *Bloch's* Schelomo . . . John Ardoin, "When Music Is Special, Aronson to Offer Beloved 'Schelomo'" *Dallas Morning News,* 4 March 1984, 1C.

57 *"a city of some culture and some distinction"* "Oral Memoirs of Daniel Ari Sternberg."

58 *two Jewish boys came to Lev, asking for help.* Details about Mr. Aronson's young students in Riga, as well as his trip to Paris, Berlin, and back to Latvia, are contained in drafts for Mr. Aronson's autobiography, *Aronson Uncollected Papers.* The first two students are referred to as Golden and Manevich in Mr. Aronson's notes. The handicapped child is called Bobby Levinson.

60 *"the little Mozart."* The child is referred to as Bavinka Neuhaus in *Aronson Uncollected Papers.* Bernard Press gives the name of the child as Chason. See *The Murder of the Jews in Latvia, 1941–1945,* p. 17.

62 *Hans Bottermund.* Mr. Bottermund's letters are in the possession of John Sharp, principal cellist of the Chicago Symphony. Hans Bottermund and his wife remained in Berlin throughout the war, experiencing considerable hardship. After the war Bottermund had the Guarnerius transferred to another bank in Copenhagen. Before Bottermund's death in 1949, he received the following letter from Furtwängler, dated 16 March 1949: "As I hear, you have for some time been seriously ill. It has pained me not to see you in your usual place at work. Hopefully, with good care, you will return soon since the orchestra needs its fine concertmaster." In 1951 Bottermund's widow sold the instrument with the hope that it would go to a cellist rather than a museum.

62 Furtwängler. See Sam H. Shirakawa, *The Devil's Music Master: The Controversial Life and Career of Wilhelm Furtwängler* (New York: Oxford University Press, 1992).

65 *He remembered the city as a Mecca* . . . Lev Aronson's description of Berlin, conversation with John Sharp, December 2007.

66 *"And why have you come back to this future inferno?"* Draft for autobiography, *Aronson Uncollected Papers*.

66 *his recordings on the Amati* . . . Janos Starker heard Lev Aronson's recordings on radio before the war. See *The World of Music According to Starker* (Bloomington: Indiana University Press, 2004), pp. 97–98.

66 *Leo Blech*. Story of Lev Aronson's audition with Leo Blech is drawn from Dennis Rooney, "Free Spirit," *The Strad*.

67 *25 Jauniela*. Lev Aronson's address, Latvian phonebook, April 1940: Arnovs Levs Cellosts Jauniela 25 Nbr 23080.

68 *"black on white, bearing the letters: C.D."* Description of the transition from Soviet occupation and the first days of Germany occupation is drawn from drafts of Mr. Aronson's autobiography, *Aronson Uncollected Papers*.

69 *"cannon futter"* Sasha Semenoff, *Don't Let This Happen Again*, privately published memoir.

WITHOUT AN INSTRUMENT

81 *"personal servants"*. . . *"phenomenally fast"* Personal details of the German occupation, life in the Riga Ghetto, in the camps, and activities after liberation are drawn from the typescript notes dated 9 May 1956 and 18 May 1956, *Aronson Uncollected Papers*. I am also indebted to several histories and memoirs. These include Ezergailis's *Latvia: The Missing Center* and Steimanis's *History of Latvian Jews*, Gertrude Schneider's three books: *Journey into Terror: The Story of the Riga Ghetto* (Westport, CT: Praeger Publishers 2001), *Muted Voices: Jewish Survivors of Latvia Remember* (New York: Philosophical Library, 1987), and *The Unfinished Road: Jewish Survivors of Latvia Look Back* (New York: Praeger, 1991), as well as Max Kaufmann's *Die Vernichtung der Juden Lettlands; Churbn Lettland* (Munich: privately published, 1947); Boris Kacel, *From Hell to Redemption* (Boulder: University Press of Colorado, 1998); Josef Katz, *One Who Came Back: The Diary of a Jewish Survivor*, translated by Hilda Reach (New York: Herzl Press and Bergen-Belsen Memorial Press, 1973); Frida Michelson, *I Survived Rumbuli*, translated and edited by Wolf Goodman (New York: Holocaust Publications) 1979; Max Michelson, *City of Life, City of Death* (Boulder: University Press of Colorado, 2004); Bernard Press, *The Murder of the Jews in Latvia, 1941–1945* (Evanston: Northwestern University Press, 2000); Jack Ratz (New York: Shengold Publishers, 1998); Sasha Semenoff, *Don't Let This Happen Again*, privately printed 1983; Alfred Winter's *The Ghetto of Riga and Continuance, 1941–1945*, privately published, 1998.

84. *allowed half the rations* . . . See Steimanis's *History of Latvian Jews*, p. 134.

85. *"Things were not yet desperate."* The description of the early days of the Riga Ghetto and the performance of the Tchaikovsky Piano Trio is drawn from "A Ring to Remember," *West Virginia University News*, 13 November 1983, *Panorama*, p. 9; Robert Fullerton, "You can Survive Almost Anything but a Bullet," *West Virginia University Magazine*, Spring 1973, pp. 2–10; and conversation with Catherine Godes, 10 September 2007. Not long after the concert, Mr. Godes, like many young people in the ghetto, had a ring made from scrap material. The opening notes of the Tchaikovsky trio were engraved on his ring, which survived the war. Mr. Godes kept the ring for the rest of his life. Max Kaufmann described the concert in "Art in the Riga Ghettos and Concentration Camps": "Commandant Roschmann and his staff (Gymnich and Bucholz) also came to the concert . . . " (translation by Laimdota Mazzarins). In Mr. Kaufmann's memory the cellist's name was Temko.

LEADING TO RUMBULA

90. *Ausekla iela, Number 3.* Anita Kugler presents a good description and history of the enterprise in *Scherwitz : der Jüdische SS-Offizier* (Köln: Verlag Kiepenheuer & Witsch, 2004).

94. *Fritz Scherwitz.* See Anita Kugler, *Scherwitz, Der Judische SS-Offizier* (Köln: Verlag Kiepenheuer and Witsch, 2004); Alexander Levin, "The Jewish SS Officer," in *The Unfinished Road* pp. 67–79; Jack Ratz, Endless Miracles, pp. 43–48. Lev Aronson also sketched a portrait of Scherwitz in his memoir, *Aronson Uncollected Papers.* After the war Scherwitz changed his name and fled to the west, claiming he was Jewish. He worked for counterintelligence until 1948, when he was recognized in Munich by a survivor of the Riga Ghetto. He was accused of shooting three Jewish prisoners at Lenta. After three trials and three appeals, he was sentenced to six years in prison. He served four years, from 1950–1954, and died in 1966.

96. *Anything valuable . . . was wrapped in linen sacks* . . . Description of burying valuables is drawn from Frida Michelson, *I Survived Rumbuli*, p. 72. Max Kaufmann also writes about it in *Die Vernichtung der Juden Lettlands*, p. 125.

AFTER RUMBULA

116 *"swimming in blood like the ghetto!"* Lev Aronson's parents died in Rumbula Forest. According to most recent estimates, approximately 27,800 Jews were killed in the ghetto, on the roads, and in the killing pits at Rumbula between November 30 and December 8, 1941. This figure includes Latvian Jews from the Riga Ghetto as well as 942 German Jews who arrived at Riga station on the morning of November 30. See Leo Dribins, Armands Gutmanis, Margers Vestermanis, *Latvia's Jewish Community: History, Tragedy, Revival* (Riga: conference paper) November 2001.

117 *Sarah Rashina.* See Ilona Brege, *Cittautu Muziki Latvija,* p. 159 and Josifs Steimanis, *History of Latvian Jews,* p. 113.

117 *"It was said the old queen . . ."* Conversation with Deborah Shelkan Remis. According to Dr. Remis, Sarah Rashina played an Amati violin that was confiscated in Riga in 1941.

118 *"one of the Arajs men, like the pied piper. . ."* The guard is identified as Arajs Kommando, Lieutenant Alberts Danskorps, in Testimony by Benjamin Edelman, Raul Hilberg, *Perpetrators* (New York: Aaron Asher Books, 1992), pp.100–101.

118 *Lev was no longer part of the Jewish leadership.* According to some survivors, Lev lost his post because he didn't allow a group of Jews from another workstation to enter Ausekla on the night before the first killings at Rumbula (perhaps under orders). According to another survivor, he saved lives of many women by having them assigned to his workshops. In his own archive, he simply says that he was demoted. For dispute concerning Lev Aronson's demotion, see Anita Kugler, *Scherwitz, Der Jüdische SS-Offizier* as well as Max Kaufmann, *Die Vernichtung der Juden Lettlands;* and Sonja Ludsin, "So Many Miracles," in Gertrude Schneider's *Muted Voices,* p. 209.

118 *Rudow.* According to the typescript notes, *Aronson Uncollected Papers,* Rudow remained in Riga with the Germans after the Jews were transported to Stutthof and, when the Germans fled, he waited for the Russian liberation. Then he was denounced as a German spy and sent to Siberia; later he emigrated to Israel. See Anita Kugler, *Scherwitz, Der Jüdische SS-Offizier* and Max Kaufmann, *Die Vernichtung der Juden Lettlands.*

119 *Richard Dannler.* Nuremberg Document NO-5124 (Jerusalem: Yad Vashem Archives).

121 *"Abram Schapiro . . ."* Sasha Semenoff, *Don't Let This Happen Again* and conversations with Sasha Semenoff, April 24–26, 2006.

121 *Percy Brand.* Gertrude Schneider, *Journey Into Terror,* pp. 53–59 and p. 97. For detailed description of music in the Riga Ghetto, see

Peter Springfield, "Music in the Ghetto," *Muted Voices* as well as Max Kaufmann, *Die Vernichtung der Juden Lettlands*, p. 242.

122 *"When I play it, I play it in memory..."* Wayne Lee Gay, "Lev Aronson Remembers," *Fort Worth Star Telegram*, 23 February 1984.

122 *"To really respond..."* John Ardoin, "When Music Is Special, Aronson to Offer Beloved 'Schelomo'," *Dallas Morning News*, 4 March 1984 pp. 1c and 3c.

122 *Lev's friend from the opera, Gregor Shelkan*... Gregor S., Holocaust Video Testimony 104, interviewed 22 July 1980 by Laurel Vlock (Boston: Holocaust Survivors Film Project) and Holocaust Video Testimony 921, interviewed 1 June 1987 by Samuel Kenner and Louise Goodman (Peabody, MA: North Shore Jewish Federation Holocaust Center), Fortunoff Video Archive for Holocaust Testimonies at Yale.

123 *A resistance group*... See Israel Kaplan, "Weapons in the Riga Ghetto," *Muted Voices*, pp. 25–40 and Steimanis, p. 234.

125 *rewarded an extra bowl of soup*... Max Kaufmann, Die Vernichtung der Juden Lettlands, p. 242. Mr. Kaufmann described two songs that Gregor Shelkan was known to sing: "Litwische Stetele" and "Der Becher."

126 *Jewish population of Lenta*. Anita Kugler, *Scherwitz, Der Jüdische SS-Offizier*, pp. 356–7 and Ezergailis, p. 362.

127 *There was a piano*...Max Kaufmann writes about concerts at Lenta in *Die Vernichtung der Juden Lettlands*, p. 244. Also, see Anita Kugler, *Scherwitz, Der Jüdische SS-Offizier*, p. 400; Jack Ratz, *Endless Miracles*, p. 44; and Aleksandrs Feigmanis, "Latvian Jewish Intelligentsia, Victims of the Holocaust": http://www.jewishgen.org/Latvia/LatvianJewishIntelligentsia.htm.

131 *"500,000 troops..."* "Huge Battle Rages in Baltic, Nazis Say," *New York Times*, 19 September 1944.

133 *"La Paloma."* English translation is adapted from a text by Domenico Savino.

STUTTHOF

134 *Balys Sruoga*. Author of *Dievu Miskai* (*Forest of the Gods*), translated by Ausrine Byla, excerpt in *Lituanus* (*Lithuanian Quarterly Journal of Arts and Sciences*), vol. 20, no. 4, winter 1974.

134 *"barbed-wire fences."* Abraham S. , *HVT* 615. Interview by Susan Horn, Lucille B. Ritvo, and Frances Proctor Cohen, Sept. 8 and Oct. 6, 1985. Fortunoff Video Archive at Yale.

134 *"Old-fashioned cobblestones"* and *"large, grassy plaza,"* Gertrude Schneider, *The Unfinished Road*, p. 4.

134 *"the smell of burning . . ."* Between 1939 and 1945, 115,000 prisoners
were deported to Stutthof. At least 65,000 prisoners died there. A
crematorium was built in 1942. See *The Encyclopedia of the Holocaust*,
edited by Walter Laqueur (New Haven: Yale University Press, 2001)
p. 614 and Muzeum Stutthof: http://www.stutthof.pl/en/main.htm.

135 *"a field full of huts"* Lev Aronson and Gregor Shelkan, "Der
durchgematerten Weg" (Berlin: Kultur Sektor, beim Central
Committee, c. 1947).

135 *"A student who faithfully does everything . . ."* Dennis Rooney, "Free
Sprit," *The Strad*.

140 *Lev was number 95,573.* Archives of Muzeum Stutthof.

147 *"I guarantee they're not going to call for cellists."* Gregor Shelkan,
Shelkan HVT 104.

148 *It was part of . . .* Kaufmann also writes about the trumpet signal, "the
familiar tune of the Marjacki Cloister Tower in Cracow."

SCHICHAU WERKE

149 Burggraben. Gregor Shelkan describes his own experience at the
Schichau Werke very movingly in Gregor S. HVT 104.

FINDING AN INSTRUMENT

173 a kind of "pyramid" Dr. Jack Frederick Kilpatrick, "Lev Aronson and
the Cello Are Inseparable Companions," *Dallas Times Herald*, 18
March 1956, p. G.3.

176 *"In ein Gewebe wanden . . . "* Lines from "Des Menschen Herz" by
Johann Gottfried Herder are translated by Brita Santamauro.

178 *In another version . . .* Story told by Larry Wilke may be a
reconstruction and welding together of all the stories of cellos that
passed through Lev Aronson's hands.

179 *"Soviet girls, blouses bulging . . ."* Czeslaw Milosz describes a similar
scene novelistically in *The Seizure of Power*, translated by Celina
Wieniewska (New York: Criterion, 1955), pp. 119–120.

180 *"I'd like to talk to you. . . ."* Jack Sheridan, "Cellist is Reborn: Lewis
Incident Stirs Memory of Dark Past," *Lubbock Avalanche-Journal*,
1959, pp. 4–5.

180 *Some of the survivors from Lenta . . .* See Boris Karel, p. 273, for
mention of his reunion with Lev Aronson and Gregor Shelkan: "On
their way to Schlactensee to seek asymlum."

181 *"The joy of freedom . . ."* Aronson speech to United Jewish Appeal,
Waldorf-Astoria, 1948, *Aronson Uncollected Papers*.

181 *Lev and Shelkan began to collaborate in a new way.* Lev Aronson
and Gregor Shelkan were taken under the wing of Harold Fishbein,

director of the two Jewish DP Camps in Berlin: Schlachtensee and Tempelhof. Three compositions by Lev Aronson and Gregor Shelkan were published by the Kultur Sektor beim Central Committee, Berlin, c. 1947.

182 *Amati's "mathematically derived" forms* . . . Cozio.com: Violins, cellos & double bases made by Nicolò Amati, http://www.cozio.com/ Luthier.aspx?id=16, 13 September 2006.

183 *"made a furtive trip to Munich"* From unpublished papers of Birdie Shelkan.

183 *Eugenie Litvinova.* Eugenie Makhotina Litvinova studied in the Imperial Ballet School in St. Petersburg. She married a general in 1913 and moved to Estonia, where she founded her own ballet school. After her husband died she emigrated to Germany.

184 *"little short of perfection . . ."* "Palestine Players End Tour in Egypt," *New York Times,* 5 November 1940.

184 *"I played for the people . . ."* Aronson, speech to United Jewish Appeal.

184 *In the recitals* . . . "World Famous Cellist Greets DP Pupil," *USNA News,* 22 April 1948.

185 *Walter Hamma.* instruments Conversation with Ute Brinkman, April 2004: "mostly the instruments that were in the galleries and therefore rescued before the bombing were saved. Many church organs survived that way—they were brought underground and put in bunkers."

187 *"dependent upon United Services for New Americans . . ."* for the period from April 1948 through September 1948, I have drawn material from Archive: USNA (United Service for New Americans) case file # J3749.

187 *Paperweight.* Conversation with Craig Casper, 23 January 2004.

187 *Lev was frustrated.* See Jack Sheridan, "Lewis Incident Stirs Memory of Dark Past."

188 *cello made by Honoré Derazey.* Conversation with David Caron, 6 January 2004.

188 *"in America they didn't want serious music"* Conversation with Nina Fevola, December 2006.

189 *Piatigorsky arranged auditions* . . . See "Lev Aronson Wants City Full of Cellists," *Dallas Morning News,* 23 July 1950.

189 *Two offers came in* . . . See Olin Chism, "The Incredible Story of Lev Aronson."

189 *Antal Dorati.* See Dennis Rooney, "Free Spirit," *The Strad.*

189 *Someone had offered him* . . . Letter to William Rosenwald, 22 September 1948, United Services to New Americans, case file J–3749.

EPILOGUE

191 *Clarence Draggert*. "Rare Cello Brought Here by Aronson," *Dallas News*, 31 May 1959.

191 *"About three years after the instrument was finished . . ."* E. Polonaski, ed., "A Valuable Violoncello," *The Violin Times*, 15 July 1898, http://www.cozio.com/instrument.aspx?id=1288, 20 January 2009

192 William de Vries. Correspondence with William de Vries, June 2005.

193 *Amnon Weinstein*. "Yidl mitn fidl," *The Jerusalem Post*, July 28, 2005, and "The Melody Plays On," *Yad Vashem Online Magazine*, Galia Limor, 2004. Conversation with Amnon Weinstein, 22 May 2005. "I can definitely say this violin was played on in the worst conditions . . ." "The Story of the Violins of the Holocaust," lecture by Amnon Weinstein.

193 *"a piano was thrown from a window. . ."* See Henry M. Holocaust Video Testimony 932, interviewed 2 April 1987 by Dana Kline and Vivian Perlis (New Haven: Video Archive for Holocaust Testimonies at Yale, 1987).

195 *a German historian* . . . Conversation with Wolfgang Eichwede, 11 February 2008.

Acknowledgments

My plans for this book began several years ago, when I heard a version of Mr. Aronson's story from the violin maker Larry Wilke. I submit it with the deepest humility. As Czeslaw Milosz put it, "The past is *inaccurate*. Whoever lives long enough knows how much what he had seen with his own eyes becomes overgrown with rumor, legend, a magnifying or belittling hearsay." Stories change many times in the telling, yet we persevere in the task of sifting through the details in order to enlarge understanding and knowledge. The work I have written is based primarily on papers, photographs, scrapbooks, and documents. I am indebted to Mr. Aronson's stepdaughter, Cheryl Surana, who has graciously shared these materials with me. I also want to thank Marina Mikhailets, music librarian at the State Library, Riga; V. Petersone and S. Šrēdere at Latvijas Valsts Vēstures Arhīvs; Margers Vestermanis, director of the Jewish Museum of Latvia; Gunnar M. Berg and Leo Greenbaum at the YIVO Institute; Romuald Drynko, dyrektor, Danuta Drywa, and Marcin Owsinski at Muzeum Stutthof; Bret Werb, musicologist, and Peter Black, historian, at USHMM; Yitzhak Gal, archivist, Kibbutz Shefayim; Maurice Klapwald, Slavic reference librarian, and Janis Kreslins, researcher, at New York Public Library; Roberta Saltzman and Amanda Seigel, Dorot Jewish Division, New York Public Library; Franklin Robinson, archives technician, Smithsonian, National Museum of American History; Tina Murdock, music librarian, Andrew Anderson, fine arts librarian, and Mike Miller, special collections librarian in the Texas History Division of the Dallas Public Library; Deborah Tobias at the Dallas Jewish Historical Society; Ellen Kuniyuki Brown, associate director and archivist of the Texas Collection, Baylor University; Sara Brewton, assistant to the dean at Baylor's School of Music; Allison Rata, music, theater, and dance librarian at the Hamon Arts Library, Meadows School of the Arts, SMU; Arian Sheets, curator of stringed instruments, National Museum, South Dakota; Suzanne Eggleston Lovejoy, public service librarian at Yale University Music Library; Joanne Rudof, archivist of the Fortunoff Video Archive; Tatjana Lorkovic, curator of Slavic and Eastern European Collections, Sterling Memorial Library; and Susan Thompson, curator, Collection of Musical Instruments at Yale.

I could never have conceived of this project without the support of my husband, Jonathan Brent, and our children, Benjamin, Jesse, and Jennie, whose musical education brought me back to my own. At different stages of my research, the following people have been generous with encouragement, expertise, and time: Paula Eisenstein Baker, Ute Brinkmann, Rabbi Herbert Brockman, David Caron, Craig Zinn Casper, Jim Denton,

Evan Drachman, Wolfgang Eichwede, Ann Ellis, Arkady Fomin, Shirli Gilbert, Catherine Godes, Lois Gordon, Jim Johnson, Joyce Jones, Kurt Kaiser, Ted Karp, Harvey Klehr, Lelde Kalmite, Philip Kass, Dorothea Kelley, Lee Koonce, Anita Kugler, Jennifer Lang, Eliot Lefkowitz, James Loeffler, Philip Margolis, Pearce Meisenbach, Roz and Rabbi Michael Menitoff, Michael Milburn, Edite Muizniece, Larry Palmer, Rabbi James Ponet, Karen Pritzker, Dace Rudzitis, Deborah Shelkan Remis, Maurice Samuels, Sasha Semenoff, Carla Shapreau, John Sharp, Jeffrey Solow, Billy Sparks, Janos Starker, Vadim Staklo, Nechama Tec, Helen Spitzer Tichauer, Willem de Vries, Amnon Weinstein, Lucille and Henry Wolf, and Alexandra Zapruder. I want especially to thank Mr. Aronson's first wife and his cousin Filip Aronson for their willingness to share what they remember from well over half a century ago. Five translators have shepherded me through this project: Britta Santamauro (German), Edward Stankiewicz and Marina Kostalevsky (Russian), Solon Beinfeld (Yiddish), and Janis Kreslins (Latvian). I'm especially grateful to James Atlas and Robin Straus, whose belief in the project, confidence, and patience have been sustaining. I also want to thank Lauren LeBlanc, Lukas Volger, Nataša Lekić, Erin Slonaker, Anna Bliss, and Sara Stemen for the thoughtful care they've given to this project.

By far the most important source for this book has been a folder that was stored among Mr. Aronson's loose papers. It contains thirty-one pages of typed notes, dated in two places: May 9, 1956, and May 18, 1956, and seven pages of accompanying source materials, dated October 15, 16, and 17, 1956. For the most part, the notes zigzag through the years 1939 to 1948, with whole blocks of remembered conversation and description of various places—Riga, Riga Ghetto, Ausekla, Kaiserwald, Lenta, Stutthof, Burggraben, Gotentov, Liegnitz, Berlin, and New York—as well as thoughts about music and survival. The notes are precise and include narrative passages sometimes written in the first person and sometimes in the third. There's no doubt Mr. Aronson worked with someone who asked excellent questions. While I don't know the identity of that person, I'm completely indebted to the work since the meticulous details of those notes provide an essential structure for much of this book. The irony has not escaped me: this project began with my curiosity of how instruments pass from one owner to another, but it has developed because of the way a fragment of writing has changed hands.